HELLISH INC

HELLISH INC

DAVID ADAMSON

Library of Congress Control Number: 2023904137

ISBN: 978-1-960093-18-9   (Paperback)
ISBN: 978-1-960093-29-5   (Hardcover)
ISBN: 978-1-960093-19-6   (eBook)

Printed in the United States of America

The Nautilus

ACKNOWLEDGMENT

I want to thank some important people in my life.

My oldest son Samuel
My daughter Jasmine
My youngest son Joshua

A friend who tirelessly listened to me in my darkest moments. "Aaron Webb".

Lastly, I want to say thanks to the spirit that moved me to write.

PROLOGUE

Locked up for eternity

I am in chains, locked in a cell with only the light shining from one barred window. All at once the heavy door to my cell thrusts open. My master has brought two more specimens. They are tossed carelessly into my grasp, a man and woman. Naked. Bruised. Bloodied. Scared. I strike the man nearly knocking the life out of him. I grasp the woman and throw her onto my bed. She looks horrified. I do not see her; I do not see the life she once had. I do not feel her pain, I do not sense her passion. I shove a strong sharp-clawed hand into her chest. The light goes out of her eyes. I howl! I pull from her chest her beating heart. It stops beating. I rip it open, that hurts me! I reach inside and fix the mistake that was made. That hurts me! I close the heart with needle and thread. That scares me! The sewing resembles writing. I thrust the heart back into her chest. I need a rib: so, I now kill the man for his rib to fix her chest, and close it. I strike her chest so! The heart starts to beat again. I fall to the floor exhausted and await her life to return. Her eyes open. That scares me! Then the light returns to her eyes. That scares her! She screams and jumps up. She does not see me! She runs to the window. I cannot reach, my master made the chains too short! A beautiful bird sees her, she clings to it and it lifts her to heavens.

Now I scream. I wail, I beat my fists onto my bed where she once lay. Her world shakes and moves to the beat of my fists, but she thinks not of me, or of my repair. I become exhausted. I fall to sleep on my bed. When I awake the man is gone. I am sitting on my cell. I am in chains in my cell. All at once the heavy door to my cell is thrust open. My master has brought me two more specimens. I am locked up for eternity.

04/05/16 04:00

Lightning spills out across the blackened sky. A million tiny lights appear in the wake of the great spark. Eyes, every one of them. Ghostly figures moving to and fro. Lightning again on the left clearly defining the outline of a *Hells Angel.* The steam drifts from him. His blackened soul steals the light from my sight. As do all the other *Hells Angels* that are now filling the sky above earth. There is a fierce pull on the atmosphere, everywhere in the sky, and like a bubble bursting. A crack, in the very air, in front of me, opens. Without effort, an *Angel of Heaven* steps out. The atmosphere shuts behind her. The realization is immediate. The darkened sky is full of *Hells Angels*, full of *Angels from Heaven.* It is the most unbelievable sight the Earth has been witness to ever, and Evermore, there will be a battle till the end.

The Angels from Heaven are impossible to look upon. God's power is in their wings. Every move is effortless, their armor is Gods own pure love. Their sword and shield appear as lightning and water. Long blonde hair stream from their heads, beautiful faces all, eyes of blue diamond. The Hell's Angels emit only steam and smoke. There is a strange bluish vapor leaking from their eyes, eyes of the blackest coal. Their wings have the power of Hell! The skin encrusted on their body was baked on. when first created, they need no armor. The darkened sky now full of Angels. God's Angels, Hell's Angels, too numerous to count. The feeling is, there are more of them, than all the grains of sand, on all the beaches on the Earth. The most awesome sight ever assembled.

The reason, me. My failed attempt to save one Angel of God, thousands of years ago. I am a Hell's Angel. I am made of hate, my soul burns in my head. I envisioned the beginning of a way to find acceptance in the sight of God. I ended up being hunted by both Heaven and Hell. Hunted by Hell hounds, and every Angel God could send. I found out stealing some of God's power, creates a vacuum in both Heaven and Hell. The vacuum opens a portal between them, and thus, man was able to finally glimpse what he was never supposed to envision. Man's armies probed and struck out in all manner of transport into heaven and hell. Causing every covenant ever proclaimed by God to be rescinded. So, here we are, looking at every Angel ever made by the heart of God, and forged in the fires of Hell.

I hang in the air effortlessly. A vapor emitted from my eyes allows me to see clearly in the dark as through it were brightest day. Steam and smoke drift from my body, as water vapor cannot settle on my flesh. It has been burned by the fires of hell. Tiny particles in the air burn off me, they ignite and wisps of smoke drift. I hate all this world, all that are alive, all that are dead. I hate myself. Sometimes I strike my body, opening a wound that would kill anything! It does not kill me! I am Fucking dead, Dead to the world, Dead to God, Dead to Hell; I'm fucking Dead to Me. I am so Goddamn dead, the dead in Hell fear me! When I move through Hell, the dead lost souls moan at my sight, and cower. I hate them, I hate Hell, I hate myself. I fly up towards the smoke and orange tinted atmosphere of Hell. My wings flash, a portal opens, I slip through.

Hell can't hold me! My wings have a power no Hell hound, or Angel from God can catch or escape. I use this power to confuse and distract all in heaven, on earth, or even, in Hell. If I meet an Angel from Heaven, I scream and fly at it! God has made the wings on every angel from heaven indestructible. However, the angel itself can be killed if I am skillful enough. The twist in all of this is that everyone has an Angel; even angels have an angel, to offer protection from attack. This is why when we fight, we fight as two always. The fight is twice as dangerous for both Heaven and Hell. God's Angel wings are indestructible, Hell's Angel wings are able to teleport through a portal between Hell and Heaven anywhere, anytime, instantly. Thus, enabling me to avoid almost any attack, it's Fucking awesome! Mostly, I like to tangle with an Angel, then disappear, then reappear, and nearly kill it! Just for *shits n' giggles.* I'm Fucking dead, remember? I get being dead. Now it's everyone else's turn to get it.

Now, I cross over from Hell to the Earth. The portal opens, I drift out. The portal shuts. Nothing can get in or out through it except a *Hell's Angel.* When I glimpse my protector Angel, I try to kill the fucking thing! For real, it had better be able to withstand my abuse, or God's Angels will surely end the fucking thing. I drift through the dark night sky over a city of at least a half a million people. What the fuck! It's Kandahar. These people are always at war. The armies of man move back and forth across the desert and in the mountainous areas. They kill each other here, year after year, for thousands of years. Man, his power, his arrogance, his greed, and his lust. What a tool in the hands of an Angel of Hell. When Evermore arrives and the Angels from **Babylon** rise, all man's power will be swept away as easily as kicking apart a campfire. Man's power has always been an illusion in order to capture as many souls from God as possible. Fuck man! Fuck God! Fuck me! I'm going to kill something tonight!!

Smoke and steam drift from me! I can see for over 50 miles in any direction, vapor pouring from my eyes would kill any man, but it enables me to see. It protects my eyes from Hell fire, and God's Angels' armor. Just the glistening from Gods' pure love off an Angel will blind anything except me. A Hellhound, a fury, a demon, all fucking useless against the armor. I see I have been followed by another Hell's Angel. It floats off to my right and lower. If I cannot find what I'm looking for, I will settle for killing that thing. We fight together, we fight each other, and we fight for Hell. Wait, the atmosphere is pulling us, this is the sign I have been waiting for. A large bubble emerges, the air splits, and the noise is deafening. Out steps 14 of Gods Angels. The atmosphere snaps shut; they hang in the air effortlessly. This is the going to be a good fucking fight; this is going to test that thing down there and our protector Angels. Hell, and Heaven are going to feel the pain tonight, I guarantee it. I hate those people down there, I hate those Angels, I hate myself, I'm going to kill everything here tonight, even if I have to kill myself to get it done. I've been a fixer for Hell for a long time. If I have got to be replaced; Hell is going to rebel against Earth and Heaven.

Angels from God have eyes of the best blue diamond. Their golden hair streams from their heads like golden silk, long, very fine threads of gold. God's armor is all about an Angel from head to toe. Here and there, there are beads of holy water; their hands have a white silk glove. Their feet have a thin sheep skin slipper. The sword is as a bolt of lightning. The shield is a portal constructed by God to hold an endless supply of saltwater. A Hell's Angel cannot penetrate it no matter how he tries. The sword can cut limbs off with a single blow, or completely gut the thing with a skillful twist in fight. The wings on an Angel of God are indestructible and can serve as an added shield from a portal shifting Hell's Angel. When an Angel of God is killed, the bolt of lightning strikes out across the sky. The portal of saltwater collapses, the water pours from the sky as rain, trying to do as much damage to any Hells' Angel in the area. But however: the wings remain with the Angel for a few seconds. They have a sort of 'GPS', that allows God to know precisely where the Angel is, and or where it died. God reaches across the expanses and touches the dead Angel, and the wings disappear. The power is returned to God. The dead Angel then drifts to the Heavens to appear as a faint star. Becoming part of what was, what is, and what will be. This is why, when drops of saltwater fall, they are tears from God.

06/05/16 14:00

God wasn't fooling around he designed me, God's love is so powerful it can reach into the heart of a Hellhound, causing a pain so great in the beast that its eyes change color, and its hair to lay flat on the back on its neck. The rage goes out of the thing, it changes into a tiger. To become a beast that protects its pride, forever. I am beautiful to look upon, my hair is made of golden strands, so long it nearly reaches my knees. The golden strands are forged from the very streets from Heaven. A place where all the souls that walk upon the streets, come into contact first and last with Heaven. My skin is so smooth and silky that it makes milk, whenever someone touches it; my eyes are made of blue diamond, the truest diamond ever. So, because of copper, the only metal used in the coloring of the diamond. Copper was first forged by man with gold. Copper looks just as lustrous than gold, but you must continuously polish it without stopping to keep it shinning. Gold on the other hand, polishes, and a bar of gold looks just as attractive years later, as when first polished. Both are heavy, both are soft to touch, but copper was first used to kill as a weapon. Gold was first used to lure someone, by its beauty, and then killed by the weapon copper. Blue diamond eyes can see everything in heaven, on Earth, or in Hell. My blue diamond eyes can see over 50 miles, in every direction. In darkness, smoke, and in Hell. I can tell your truest intentions. I can feel every fiber of your being; I can look into your heart. Touch your pain and absorb it.

Standing here, just after I stepped through a portal from Heaven. The atmosphere snapped shut behind me. I hang effortlessly, the air all around me is filled with a sharp tension, never felt by any Angel from Heaven. I gaze everywhere, Angels' everywhere! OH My God, this cannot be. Before me, an Angel from Hell, smoke and steam drift from him. But what, the air is full of them. Full of God's Angels, Full of Hell's Angels. Oh my God, I can see into the heart of a Hell's Angel. This is dangerous, the hate, the rage, and the pain, the suffering. The hate, I have never felt hate like this. I didn't know there was hate like this. God never told me about this hate. Why haven't the things in the air tried to kill me? Or the other Angels from Heaven, why has nothing moved, why haven't I moved yet? What is going on? We have been sent here to bring an end, to all that is, all that has, and all that will be, for Evermore. Why haven't I struck the thing before me, why haven't my wings moved? My wings are what make me an Angel, an Angel from God. God's power is in my wings, they are indestructible. God's power is, was, and always will be. I can't be here floating effortlessly, over the Earth, with all the Angels, without God's power. What is going on? I cannot feel my hair drifting, I cannot feel my sword, or the power of the portal holding the saltwater. I cannot feel my beautiful body; I've looked upon myself so many times, standing nude before a mirror. The love of God all about me, my beautiful body so strong and graceful in the bright sunshine. Long blonde hair, blue diamond eyes, skin like milk, and the taste of me is the same as the best honey made in a honeycomb. Made of milk and honey, protected by God's armor and given God's own power in the form, of wings. This is what is needed to create an Angel of God. With the wings I can fly through a portal to earth. I can fly through a portal to Hell; I was built to come into contact with, and survive any insult, thrown at me by a demon, fury, Hell Hound, and survive any attack by a Hells' Angel. But I know I can be killed, many of us have been. The lights in heaven are there to remind me of just how many of us have tried to defeat Hell's rage. I always wondered if I would join them in Heaven and shine a light in the night. No matter how seemingly insignificant that light may be. When I fly straight through Heaven, I can be as a wind touches leaves on a tree. I can be as the light from the sun of a flower, or I can be as the sound of bells ringing in the distance. The ones in Heaven see me, and are moved to tears of joy, and shameless abandon. They begin to dance and sing. It's as if life has just begun, and the first promise God made was: a brand-new day.

I fly effortlessly through Heaven and pass gracefully through a portal over Earth, anytime, anywhere. I fly with a protector Angel always at my side, I love life, I love Heaven, and I love all of the people of Earth and their souls. I love Angels, the things made by God are not visible by mortals, they cannot see Heaven, and they cannot see Hell. They can only catch a glimpse of spirits, and sometimes they can see an

Angel. Be touched by one. Sometimes they can talk to us, and us to them. Always mortals have an Angel by their side until death. That is Gods second promise. Amazingly it has happened that an Angel feels so strongly for a mortal, that it gives up its existence in the moment before the mortal will die. And may even die in the arms of a mortal. Angels from God are instructed not to be so foolish, as the one thing God has warned is: if when the Angel dies before God can recover the power in the wings, the wings may be stolen by a mortal. Or worse a demon or Hell's Angel. I am an Angel from Heaven, I am the most powerful thing God has ever, will ever, and ever will be. I am more powerful than even the Fixer Angel from Hell. The only weakness I have is, my body cannot handle moving between Heaven, Earth and Hell. Therefore, I must pass through a bubble in a portal; I can create anytime, anywhere, with just a flash from my wings. This portal opening and closing pulls at the atmosphere, giving warning of my arrival to any messenger from Hell. And thus, I have no chance of a surprise attack, and can be attacked with no notice once stepping out. I must fully have trust in Gods armor, every time I travel. Thus, God has put all his trust in every Angel he creates. God gave me a sword made of lightning that can cut out the guts of a demon or fury. The sword can cut through the toughest hide of a Hell's Angel, and can even cut off its arms, legs, or even better, cut off its wings. So, I can watch it fall back to Hell where it came from. Also, God gave me a shield, the shield itself is designed to hold a whole Sea of saltwater. So powerful the shield is, any strike possible by a Hell's Angel is useless to harm the shield or myself, shielded by the blow. God's promise is to protect me with his love, to protect with the ability to move through the air as wind or a breeze and create a stairway to Heaven for souls to tread upon. To be received at the Gates of Heaven. That is why my hair is golden, made from the very gold from the streets of heaven to tread upon. Because of God's promise, because of Gods will, because of Gods protection, because of Gods trust. I will promise to protect and trust every soul ever created. This statement is what every Angel of Heaven must state before God when created, because it contains the four truths: Will, Promise, Trust and Protection. God wasn't fooling around when he designed Angels, Angels are Gods only hope for the souls on Earth to get to Heaven, and not fall to Hell. Where they can be turned in demons and Hell's Angels. Where the balance between Heaven and Hell becomes Hell bound, and out of control. If this happens, God will move Heaven closer to Earth, God will become enraged at all those in Hell, and God will throw every Angel he can and will ever make straight at the heart of Hell. Trying to kill Hell itself and losing his only hope for love, peace, trust, and truth, to destroy Hell and everything along with it.

07/05/16 20:30

I look to my right, then left, there are fourteen of us, Heaven's beautiful Angels. seven of us and seven protector Angels. We had traced the Fixer Angel to this location, I have a shrewd, sagacious plan worked out previously with the other six of us. We will make an attack here, when the Fixer Angel portals: four of us will be waiting in Hell for him when he slips, If we can divide his team, he will lose, or we will die trying. Too much damage is being wrought here in the desert areas. The thing is lately the Fixer has had a spree of kills; we have been told to be on guard for some sort of new power the Fixer maybe using. As the kills were without much contention. If such a skill is assumed by the Fixer, God can equal it. But however; God needs to know the root of the power being used. We have been sent to find the root of it, kill the Fixer, or die trying. Will, Promise Trust and Protection.

The smoke and stream remain, but a flash, the Fixer and follower disappear. Two of us move to where he was last, two of us move to the location of the follower, four of us go to Hell, this requires a portal. The fixer will be alerted to the arrival. So now we use our well laid out plan. Those four will not step out of bubble but will return here. The four of us left will then portal through and step out 2 minutes later. The fixer should be using his new power on Angels that do not appear. Thus, we may witness this power and use our surprise entrance to watch and engage him, while not being subject to their plan. The atmosphere pulls, the four are gone, we wait. I can still sense the presence of the Fixer; the slight taste of smoke is in the air. Now it's time, we four now flash our wings, the atmosphere gives away, we each step through the bubble, we are through. Hell, this place is alive with hate. Without God's armor we would be dead instantly. I look unbelievably at the scene before me. Four of God's Angels hang in space before us, here in Hell, not moving. We all now hang here not moving, what is going on? This must be what has happened but wait. The Fixer and his follower Angels aren't moving either. They are fixed on the other four and not us. It strikes me that all eight of them are frozen somehow, like us, Hell is alive. Creatures of all manner, that aimlessly drift in Hell are moving beneath us, Funny, they don't seem to know of our arrival. One of us must make it back to Heaven. No matter what and must bring the information of this power to God. What power can freeze eight of the most powerful things God has ever created, what power can freeze the Fixer Angel, and hold us all above Hell. Concealing us in a cloak, that Hell itself cannot feel our presence. Hell is alive, Hell is like an egg, it has definite borders that encase it. This protects it from man and his intentions of power. God encased it so it would rot, but instead it thrives. It thrives because of its ability to absorb more souls from man. The souls are called lost because they are stripped of God's essence. The powerful elixir is then used to feed Hell and provide what is required to produce all the demons, furies, Hellhounds, and Hell Angels. These are all really things that do not exactly exist, they are all virtual realities. Hell has a mental arrangement that exist in Hell only. And must consume souls for power and existence, the powerful elixir produced by this essence can be saved up like memories in the brain. Then be used to produce the most horrible powerful Arch Angel or Hell's Angel.

08/05/16 23:00

The Arch Angel contains the very essence itself and the hallucinogenic properties therein; to be able to defeat an Angel completely, and utterly defeat an Angel from Heaven in combat. To understand the Hells'

Angel completely, one must become a Hells' Angel. Which is not impossible. Just a little foolish to believe, that one day you might escape Hell, God, and the deliverance of Hell. The acquisition of God's power from the essence, to become once again, in mortal condition, to then analyze the Arch Angel and its qualities. However, it could be done and for now let us consider only that it may have happened, and not dwell upon it. For an understanding will become illuminated as the events unfolding now will enlighten and illustrate. The Arch Angel is of God in 'essence' only, but a product of the mind of Hell; therefor, has only a virtual existence. The Angel of Heaven is a creation of God in the form of the indestructible wings, the golden strands from the very streets of Heaven, (this is how souls may climb the stairway to Heaven), and the lightning bolt sword, the portal of seawater (shield) and the blue diamond eyes. The blue diamond eyes pierce the mental shield of man, beast, demon of Hell, or and through any reasonable obstacle that confronts the Angel. The blue diamond has the quality of the weapon copper, which protects the Angel from Hellfire, portal through Hell, or into Heaven. Also giving an extreme quality of acuity, not found in any other gemstone. Being immersed in Hell is unbelievable, the stench of rotting corpses, both human and animal. Extremes of humidity, and aridness. Unending suffering, screams, howling, growling. The sound of chains breaking bones, and huge explosions. The acrid smell of burning flesh, plastic, rubber, wood, petrol, and any number of hallucinogens. The last of which is important, because without the hallucinogenic effect on the very mind of Hell, it could not envision and establish control of the virtual quality of the immensely powerful Hell's Angel. And, most importantly, the one and only Fixer Angel. The Fixer Angel is such a complicated, ambiguous equivocal virtual being, that only one may exist in universe at any one time. This Fixer Angel is Hells' antidote to Gods' control over Hell itself. The Fixer Angel must be considered in two ways and is always trying to control two emotions of opposite and equally disturbing outcomes at once. Hence its ability to fight on two fronts at once. And hinder 4 times the power thrown at it. And now the thing has figured a way to control time and dimensional space in a fixed frame, within its vision. If the area is large, the Fixer spreads this range by using the other Hells' Angel's virtual interaction to Hell to spread the effect as far as the Fixer can in time and space. In order to gain an advantage over any combatant he views as a threat. This is the very effect it used to gain leave from its cell in Hell when it was first envisioned by Hell to gain control over the coming Christ of God. Both went terribly wrong, and the Fixer Angel is the result of a wrong never to be foretold by God or Hell, because of the very equivocal nature of the Fixer and Christ. In both cases we are considering a completely emphatic messiah. Capable of saving Heaven, Hell, or the Earth in two completely different directions of discovery while, maintaining authority of being.

09/05/16 22:30

Now we look at how the Fixer escaped from his cell, while in unbreakable chains, set upon him by God and Hell itself. The Fixer realized that there was a moment just after the heavy door to his cell pushed open, that it was actually a portal. Every time the master opened the door and tossed in two subjects, the Fixer began studying how he could take advantage of both the master and the portal. He realized that by freezing time just as the master gave him that dejected look, that was the time. The Fixer used this unique ability to reconstruct the woman's' heart once he ripped it out of her. The master, Hell, nor God knew of the Fixer's ability to freeze time and dimensional space. What an un-erudite condition for Hell or God to be in. For the very existence of knowledge is broken down into two senses, being able, and to know. With the Fixer locked up for eternity, God and Hell thought one of them would be first to figure out, why men idolize women, and hate themselves, for wanting to kill their own souls. When the woman wants to control the man's behavior, and sense of oneness with the world around him. If the Fixer could fix this mistake in the heart of an experienced woman, the master thought he would be the first to calculate an antidote to a possible Christ being by God. God felt that when he sent the Phoenix to rescue the woman at the barred window. The woman would return to the Earth, and with a fixed heart she would spread a sense of uncontrollable decision making among other women. Thus, stopping man from wanting to kill his own soul and starving Hell of souls ending the Fixer and the need for Christ.

The Fixer Angel, looks, feels, smells and tastes like everything in Hell. When he looks upon his master for the last time, he flashes his wings. Time and space in the immediate area freeze. The master of the portal is a mere demon, and a far inferior being to the Fixer. The demon is forced to stare at the Fixer. The demon cannot control his hatred of himself in the glare of the Fixer. Once it is of undeniable certainty the demon is going to give up its existence due to the hatred inflicted by the Angel, the Fixer Angel flashes his wings, the demon steps forward towards the Angel in utter anguish and the Fixer Angel reaches out, and with a gesture cuts the demon in two. Takes his control of the portal and pulls it toward himself. The chains are immediately dissolved by the power of the portal. The Fixer enters the portal a free Hell's Angel. Thus, becoming the absolute reason Hell has no power over or to control the virtual essence in the Fixer. A Hell's Angel with two consciences and each with the ability to conceive alterable outcomes in any instance. Literally a Hell's Angel times eight. This is how the infinity symbol came to be recognized as a sideways 8. Once freed he became infinitely endowed with the elixir in Hell. I watch intently the scene of four of God's Angels frozen before four Hells' Angels. The scene is intoxicating and poisonous at the same time. Then without warning, horribly, I see God's Angels losing their armor, as if shedding skin. All four die in an instant. Their bodies disappear in a faint wisp of smoke. Their wings flash and disappear. We flash and portal back to where we were before entering Hell, hoping to regroup, and message Heaven. Our hopes are dashed when stepping out of our bubble. We find ourselves confronted by the Fixer himself. This time there is no freezing, as he flies at us with an intuition in his head that we four are helpless to fight once shaken by the deaths of the four in Hell only moments ago. I drop straight to the Earth beneath us. The other three are immediately torn to shreds by the powerful blows from the Fixer and accompanying Angels. Lightning streaks out across the skies, and saltwater falls as rain everywhere. Lightning is not possible in Hell, and water cannot form there either. These things are only possible here in Earth. The Hells' Angels are pursuing me but instantly two of them are overcome by the saltwater, they flash and disappear in order to save themselves. I fly straight at the other two using the God's tears to cover me in brilliance. I am not afraid of these things they can die too. The Fixer's protector is reached first. On a first pass my sword takes one of his wings and half an arm off. It's back to the Fires of Hell for him. Now before I commit to the final battle I flash. Emerging into Heaven, I step fourth from the bubble. No, it cannot be! The Fixer is here! In front of me, in Heaven too! I am frozen, he is frozen, most of the Heaven closet to us is frozen. I see his hate, I see his pain, I see his split personality. I am utterly ashamed by his empathy. As his conciseness enters my imagination, I lose control of my hold on reality. At once the armor on my body falls off, like shedding skin. I hang nude before this monster, I am ashamed and helpless. Surely, I will die now. He flashes and disappears. I am in Heaven, I feel like Hell.

10/05/16 22:00

I drift slowly down on to a street. In Heaven the golden streets are soft to touch flowers grow along the streets along with shrubs and fruit bearing trees. Butterflies and birds constantly amass in groups and playfully fly by. The sunlight here is splendid and feels warm on the soul. There are no true bells that ring, only sound of bells ringing in the distance to announce the passing or passage of Angels. Small sparks pass by illuminating the playfulness of animals of all types. They jump and chase the sparks. God has planned all things in Heaven to be as natural and peaceful as a summer rain while the sun still shines. Creating rainbows everywhere, and shimmering ponds, and creeks. Fish and all manner of marine life abound in these waters. Everything fells so smooth and calm even when the wind blows, and leaves kick up and dust fly's it still feels as though nothing but the stillest water you have ever seen is laying everywhere. Sometimes you can see clouds billowing up and then they part exposing Heaven's beautiful dark sky and shimmering stars in the distance along with the passing of a lunar body, shooting stars and comets, Light exists everywhere. Children run and play here and there; men and women walk amongst the children and there seems to be a careless abandon amongst all. Souls in Heaven can appear and fade at any moment. No one here has any sense of time. Time does not exist in Heaven; Times stops at Heaven's gate. Time is man's creation, Heaven and Hell can exist if there is time, ebb or flow.

Now I am standing on a street in Heaven. God's pure armor is lying around the street in front of me. My beautiful body is standing nude for the first time in a place of absolute presence, elegance and grace. I am made of milk and honey; my feet wear a thin slipper of the finest sheep skin; my hands are dressed in a white silk glove. My fine golden hair streams by my side like the beautiful mane on a fine racehorse. My blue diamond eyes do not ever fear, Angels need never tear because God's Will, Protection, Trust and Promise can never allow an Angel to feel fear and cry as a result. Tears are streaming down my face; they burn my skin. My blue diamond eyes that cannot cry are crying, I cannot stop the tears from flowing down my face. I am still holding my sword and shield; my wings are still and somehow feeling lost. I feel pain and I am ashamed at the destruction of God's armor. God will be in front of me in any moment I am so scared. My mind is racing, and I can't focus on Heaven, all I feel is the Hell that has found its way into my mind. I have been told of the Fixer of Hell, how this drug is a derivative of the souls captured in hell. A *hallucinogen* exists in the mind of the Fixer at all times allowing it to cast a perception into the conscience of another Angel of Hell or Heaven, thus creating the ability of a multi layered attack in synchronized succession without being delayed by communication. Or in the mind of a Heaven's Angel the perception of perplexing anguish. Imagine Hell in the mind of a Heaven's Angel.

Can I tolerate anything more, can I feel the breeze on my skin or hear bells ringing in the distance. I can't focus; Heaven is disappearing before my vision. I believe I will die and return God his power, I will drop my sword and shield and give up this ghost of Hell, A ghost of Hell in Heaven. I wake up at once, I stop crying immediately, God's armor rises up from the street and dances around me I feel a presence of Holiness all around. God armor once again returns to me I am saved; I alone know why. I flash my wings; I step into the bubble portal into Hell This time there is no pulling at the atmosphere no warning of my arrival will be given to any messenger of Hell. The Fixer will not know I am here at all. For the first time an Angel from Heaven is going to get some fucking revenge on this place. I will fuck up some of this place and get some answers or done trying. As I gracefully pass over the River STYX and watch the lost souls cross over, I notice souls are frater and gesturing in my direction. I spin and dive straight down, I throw down my shield onto acrid water of the STYX then landing on the shield, I surf the river: my wings are sails pushing me with ease, I force a huge plume of smoke from the river up on the banks the STYX; the acrid liquid can only exist in the canal made for it, no water can exist anywhere else in hell no matter how resilient. Thus, as the STYX rises in the atmosphere of Hell, it immediately becomes smoke and ash spills on to the banks of the canal, Wondrousness in Hell.

I am playing in the River STYX. I am the *MAKO* flying among lost souls in Hell. The answers are lying at the bottom of this awful canal of torture and suffering. I will spill all its blood onto the banks and expose the truth of the STYX to the lost souls. After all isn't that why they cross over to remain lost in Hell while they are stripped of the essence of God in their crossing? The fixer and companion Angel arrive on the other side of the STYX and stare fixedly in my direction. I am pleased by the attention, I now command. What a wonderful enticing perception to watch. An Angel of Heaven playing in the river of STYX totally unhindered by the lost souls and exposing the truth of Hell to all those who cross over and watched by the fixer and his protector.

There is a ghost of Hell in my conscience and it wants revenge. I stop; hang motionless above what was once the STYX now choked by all the ash built up while lost souls disappear at an amazing rate. The Fixer is frozen, his protector is frozen. I am not, let's play with you Fixer I flash and reappear before his eyes and flash and reappear before his protector who is falling into pieces as my sword slices through his entire body with ease. I flash; I'm gone from Hell. I must regroup my thoughts, for I cannot return to Heaven, I don't know how God will accept this reality that exist in me or if I will eventually be hunted by Heaven and Hell. My allegiance is to Heaven, but I feel like I am at home in Hell. God help me I know I must surrender for acceptance.

12/05/16 22:00

Where in Hell is Heaven, where in Heaven is Hell. Why should anyone even consider these concepts? Why does the fixer freeze its prey? How does the Fixer control two consciousness's capable of perceiving two exclusive truths? Why does the Mako fly into Hell to expose a truth? Why would I lie to tell the truth? Why would I truthfully tell you a lie? When the Fixer broke his chains and escaped from the eternal test, he became two personalities to fix the woman's heart; he needed to freeze her life for an instant to preserve the soul. Then he removed her heart and fixed the mistake, sewed it back together, fixed the damage and used his freeze to restart the heart. However, saving the soul is not supposed to be done in Hell. That is why the Fixer is so exhausted and weak afterwards. Hate and love, strong and weak, hard and soft, hot and cold, wet and dry, Heaven and Hell. Human that just leaves the Heavens and Earth. Go to Hell or come to Heaven.

A long time ago when there was no way to settle a dispute except by fire, people were less likely to lie about the truth. Today good people are making debts. with anyone in order to get what they want. Man's power is eroding the Protector Angel's power to steer him on to the path of righteousness. So many people are condemning the other that many people are becoming lost to the world and know only hate before they die or any reason. Then they fall into Hell to add their soul to Hell's Trough. Funny that a little likes the shape of the River STYX. A river where no such thing can exist. Where is the truth in Hell? Poisonous water running through Hell strips the soul of its essences and the hides the truth of Hell's thirst for salvation.

I am the Fixer; I have escaped from the great test. I can change the future; I can even change the past. I can fix anything. What in the Hell, is an Angel from Heaven doing in Hell with a ghost from Hell? This Angel was not possible at any time, except now. This must be the Angel that I stripped in Heaven. Now its portals anywhere and I cannot perceive its coming. I made the mistake that I may not be able to fix. If Heaven hunts this Angel, I will have to protect it, but I am a Fixer Angel not a Protector Angel. Hell will have to wait. I must go. I flash my wings, a ghost from Hell cannot hide from me nor can it hide from God. I portal out beside the Angel to my right with a new attitude. She is beautiful, I never noticed this before, I have never been able to look on a Heaven's Angel because of God's armor. But now I look at her beauty, long golden mane, luscious blue diamond eyes, milky skin, wings from God. I cannot freeze her, she can flash and kill me just as she did my protection, I cannot flash her my wings. I must wait to see if she will accept me or kill me, I cannot fix this. The Angel from Heaven stands by my side like a statue, strong, serene, lovely. I sense the danger and unpredictable nature of the ghost of Hell in her. When God's Angels arrive which I'm sure they will, will we fight together, will we fight for Hell? I'm already dead remember, now this beautiful Angel from Heaven has a dead soul in her consciousness. She gets being dead, but she must return to the sky to die.

15/05/16 22:30

All at once, a protector angel from Hell arrives beside the fixer. Then another protector Angel from Hell arrives beside the Angel from Heaven with the ghost from Hell in her. Then six more of

Hell's Angels and their accompanying protectors arrive. Just to the left and higher a massive bubble in the atmosphere begins to stretch the atmosphere. Heaven's Angels are coming. Immediately the Fixer freezes all the Hell's Angels so they cannot surprise attack Heaven's army. Then the bubble opens. Angels too many to count start to step forth, as they step out and take up positions, they become frozen as well. One the number of Heaven's Angels stop emerging the bubble snaps shut, what a scene there must be over one hundred of these beautiful Angels. Then comes the moment I was waiting for. I am the Fixer but now I am a Protector Angel as well, will she recognize this, or will I die and start a war no one can win. The Angel on my right now the only Angel that is not frozen steps forward. Grace will on every move she starts to dance, and everyone can hear bells ringing a light rain starts to fall. These are not God's tears this is like amidst and a light rain. Light seems to come from everywhere. Steam and light puts of smoke doubt off ever Hell's Angel. And now I see steam and small pulls of smoke from the Heaven's Angel as well she moves toward Heaven's army. I unfreeze four immediately in front of her. They move to her side they began to dance and bells sound everywhere beautifully.

I send instructions to all Hell's Angels if they move after I unfreeze, I will kill them all myself before I die here and now. I unfreeze all Angels at once. Immediately the Heaven's Angels part into two groups. The largest group maybe sixty of the estimated hundred, group up with the five that are dancing and ringing bells. The rest just hang on midair not moving. Then I move to my Angel's side and take a position to her left again. She stops dancing and looks at me I can't believe it she is crying. She throws her sword up and the lightning bolt streaks across the sky. Then she tosses her shields and the portal collapses and saltwater runs down on everyone. The Hell's Angels have been warned not to move or face certain death, so they wait and smoke some flare up and then they start to burn heavily but then the saltwater rain stops and they start to recover. She then sheds her armor, and it continues to dance without her. She began to walk toward me. She is stunningly beautiful. What is she doing? Heaven can wait, Hell can wait. Heaven's Angels are now circling around us. I can freeze them before they elect an attack and we can escape, but will she escape or will she or will she want to die to release the ghost? This Angel from Heaven stops within six inches of me. She is looking directly into my eyes crying and not nervous or trembling at all. Her breasts are just away from me, I feel warmth in my body. I feel a strange pull from her. She reaches out and caresses my head and down in my belt and takes my hand and places it on the middle of her chest!

Help! Help! Help me please she says to me Help me to go to the Heavens and take my place with the other Angels. Help me please I surrender to you, I surrender to you. All of the Angels from Hell and all of the Angels from Heaven start to chant to pledge at the same time. I will promise, trust, and protect every soul from God. Over and over on stopping, I am silent as I have my left and held in place over the heart of a gift from God. Her hand holds my hand she wants me to kill her. I take my hand that is free on my other hand I place it on my chest and for the first time I feel her skin as I place her hand on my chest. I can't believe it I feel alive, is this possible? Can it actually be possible? I am dead, dead, dead, Fucking dead to the dead! What is this, she surrenders to me, we touch the next thing I know I am not dead anymore. She says, can you return me to Heaven and release the ghost in my head. This war does not need to happen. Fixer you do not need to come here on Earth, you need to be there at the battle of evermore, only you can stop that battle. Kill me here before you die, and the great battle loses you. I hold her hand over my heart. I say I can kill you; you can kill me. But don't you realize that when the ghost entered you, I became your protector. I am the Fixer and your protector. If I kill you, I kill myself. We both fucking die. Right here, Right Now. I surrender to you just as you surrender to me. You can accept me; I can accept you Heaven and Hell can wait.

The Angels all around us are chanting the creed. They expect me to kill the gift from God. They expect to see a battle in which she dies, and the Fixer dies soon after. What they don't know is I am not dead anymore. Then I noticed that smoke no longer drift from me nor steam. My wings fall off. The Angel in front of me reaches behind her and pulls her wings off and slams them on my back. Holy shit this is not happening. Next thing an Angel from Heaven steps forward and pulls her wings off and put them on my beautiful crying Angel. That other Angel then drifts upwards to Heaven to be a light on the night sky. My Heaven's Angel says that was my Protector Angel. I am now an Angel from Hell, as are you. However, you are the Fixer and you are not dead anymore. You need to go to Heaven and save your soul or you cannot exist till the battle forevermore. You shall die and Hell will replace you. Your replacement will kill me and attack Heaven through me and a rebellion will break out. God will throw every Heaven's Angel at the heart of Hell and everything will be lost. Go save your soul I will follow you I will protect you I will promise I will trust you, I will. You will, you promise, you trust me, and you will protect me. We will be saved. God will accept you. You surrendered. I surrendered. We will be accepted. We flash. We appear in Heaven on a golden street, my feet feel the street through my soul. Finally, I am saved, she saved me.

17/05/16 23:00

I stand in Heaven on the golden streets of Heaven, I am the Fixer, a Hell's Angel, I have almost come full circle, my soul is saved but I cannot wear God's armor. I must return to Hell and cast off my beast like body and then back in Heaven I may purify my body and be able to wear the armor of God. I hear bells ringing everywhere, I fell the sun on my flesh warm and confronting I see animals and all manner of insects everywhere. Rainbows in the Heavens. My Protector Angel walks beside me. I can't know how she feels because she still is duality with a ghost of Hell in Heaven. How is this possible that I can't feel her conscience?

I have the ability to see straight through any mental defense. God, I'm the one who stripped her and her armor. I caused her duality. Hell can't hold her nor can Heaven. God will not even stand before us in Heaven, while I look like Hell and she carries a ghost of Hell. I will promise, trust and protect every soul from Heaven. I stop and turn to her. I chant the Angel's creed Bells ringing stop and she starts to chant as well. Then Angels from Heaven appear all around. They stay silent as we chant. I cannot freeze her; I could freeze the others but not her so I can't drive that ghost out of her conscience. I cannot find a way to fix this. My eyes of black coal do not hold any emotion, the vapor leaking from them is my only difference from certain destruction. We surrendered to each other, our dualities are separate, but our future is a combination.

While I chant, while she chants, I notice tears streaming down her face. I don't know why she is crying; her duality is blocking my attempt to intuition and perception. Angels from Heaven cannot cry. This Angel is crying. I stop chanting as does she I reach out for her chest I place my right clawed hand on her chest. She drops her sword, places her right hand on my horrible flesh where my hearts should be. I looked into her eyes. I see her this time, I am horrified I cannot feel this. I ripped the hearts out of so many women, when in chains and never was able to see their past lives or feel their passion. What in Hell is going on in Heaven? The ghost of Hell is killing her. When she surrendered to me the ghost began to intrude into her mental aggregate once there it began to dissemble her conscience. Now she is dying before me and I may be powerless to stop it from killing her. I call out to God. What hath thou done. Thine trap is not the end you seek. The dissembling of this Angel is also a spear to my own existence. Thou shall not change the future of thine own plan without justification before the surrender of both Heaven and Hell. Without my double duality the end of everything will, promise trust and protection of every soul is lost to both Heaven and Hell. God answer to this, God I beseech thee. God stand before us Give us the future you planned now before it's too late… please…

As I scream to the Heavens with my face turned upwards, I feel her collapse to me. I fall to the ground on my knees. A Hell's Angel on his knees begging God for help. Lightning begins to from around my beautiful Angel and protector. I feel this is the moment I cannot bear to live through. I could have been dead still. I would not feel a thing. God please she is dying, save her take me, anything she is dying. Then I notice the other Angels around us have begun to chant. Then I see bells, Angels flashing here from where we were standing just moments ago when I thought there would be a battle to the end of us for our coming together. These Hell's Angels are gathered amongst. The Heaven's Angels and are chanting as well. I am stuck by a bolt of lightning. It passes through my body and penetrates into my protectors will, is God going to kill us both here and now. How will I end this life it's only just begun? I feel like Hell again. I feel like killing everything on Heaven. I feel hate again I am the Fixer again. The lightning bolt is gone. I stagger backwards. Holy fuck the Heavens, the Heaven's wings on me are gone. Hells wings are back. My beautiful Angel stands up, skin like milk, blue diamond eyes. She is not crying anymore. She looks at me and says, God has restored the ghost of hell back to you. You are dead again. Now you know what it feels like to live and die. You are a Hell's angel, and now you are reborn.

21/05/16 21:00

I take a knee and cast my gaze downward. I speak to the Heaven's Angel before me as she picks up her sword and shield. I am the Fixer; I surrender to you. You are free from pain now and may strike me dead, dead to you, dead to Heaven and the Earth and its souls. I am dead so fucking dead, that even the lost dead souls in Hell fear my passing. I know not what I have done to earn your respect, but I surrender to you before God and his Angels. The beautiful Angel standing before me raises her sword to the Heavens before me. She says the creed I will, promise, trust and protect all Gods souls to the gates of Heaven, and now to the gate of Hell. I once was pure and only made of milk and honey. Now I have been taken by a ghost of hell, I have lived a duality I have been the Mako and attacked the River STYX in Hell itself. I have been utterly driven insane by the ghost of

Hell and finally killed by my own God. God only can kill his Angel and strip it of a duality the cause the Angel to be reborn. God has returned me my soul he has given me a choice to accept my current position as Heaven's angel or to continue as the Mako. I accept the choice is mine and I will promise, trust and protect the Mako and follow you. Fixer, I am forever more your protector. I will follow you to Hell, I will even get you a guided four if you want.

The Heaven's Angel rises up and takes the shield in her hand and holds it out in front of her and let's go of it. The shield drops to the golden street below and the portal is disintegrated by the power of redemption in the soul powered golden street, the very power of the redeemer who walks the streets of Heaven and saves the souls who enter and walk the streets of Heaven. No shield may touch the golden streets of Heaven. No salt water may fall from the skies of Heaven either. God tears only fall on Earth from the Heavens, when God's own Angels die, and God never cries in heaven ever. So now the portal is destroyed and out spills the salt water. Instantly turned into pearls. Out they pour onto the streets and everywhere else in Heaven. This is the first time ever that a shield portal has collapsed in Heaven. The first-time salt water quickly turns into an innumerable amount of the most beautiful pearls ever seen. Seeing all of the pearls spilling out into Heaven, God then opened heaven to the Earth to allow the pearls to spill into all the soft mollusks in the oceans of Earth. Proclaiming that the power of redemption has created the best beauty hidden on a shell of like beneath the oceans for man to find and give to each other. Man is to remember that giving a pearl is nothing short of the best beautifully mixture of God's tear and the power of like itself and God gives them freely to man and the whole world to express beauty and kindness amongst his kind.

As the pearls spill outward some of them come in contact with me, a Hell's Angel. They immediately explode, causing shimmering in the lights and giving off rainbow effects in the air. As fire and electricity of any kind is not possible in Heaven, just as water or any form of life is not possible in Hell. I drift upwards towards my protector Angel, a new confidence is my every move, as in hers, my duality now able to see into her conscience and perceive her very essence. She feels my intrusion into her coincidence and without hesitation, asks me to once again instill and establish the ghost of Hell into her mind, that once again the Mako may fly into Hell and be amongst the living. The Mako must have its truth and will have the truth to be known to the living and the dead. All the while I will remain your protector and reside in Hell; with you always till the battle of Evermore. Tears are once again streaming down her beautiful face, as she is feeling my hate, and my pain and suffering. I am reluctant to agree to the request as I am sure God will not intervene a second time. We are a combination now, a dual essence inside our own minds and the outcome of our combined existence is ambiguous, equivocal and will not be under the govern or influence of Heaven or Hell. The paradox may lead to the demise of us all and even before I am able to carry out the request. I am the Fixer; I am able to change the outcome of even this. I will, promise, trust and protect you, come now my protector.

Pearls are flowing everywhere; rainbows and lights of all colors are flying everywhere. The sight of a beautiful Angel of Heaven flying above the streets of Heaven with an Angel of Hell at her side is all once a perplexity and an embodiment of the combination of a double duality out of the reach of God and Hell. God touches an Angel of Heaven and that Angel moves to the side of the Mako and chants the oath to her and becomes her protector. God touches another Angel, and she flies to the side of the first protector and chants to that angel. Now the Mako are a trinity. The Fixer however, so loud that the pearls all around him shake an vibrate and two Hell's Angels fly to his side. He immediately hits them with a blow that should have killed them, but he then freezes them and strikes then on fire, but they are on Heaven and Hell fire is not allowed to be lit. Hence so a blue vapor pours off of then and their wounds heal quickly before they expire. Then the Fixer howls again and flies around the group like a wild furry and repeats the oath I will promise trust and protect all souls of God. To Heaven and Hell. Come now Mako, we have to finish this, come now Mako follow me to the gate of Hell and bring your protector with you. I will give you all a guided tour. Hell won't be your home but to truly be the Mako you must return to the River STYX and receive the truth you seek. You must receive the ghost of Hell into your conscience once more and you must commit to your child of truth.

All of the Angels begin to fly in dizzying circles in every direction around the Mako and the Fixer then, flashes and the Hell's Angels two at a time disappear, and in a synchronized movement with flash, the trinity and the fixer and his accompaniment all disappear together. Heaven now partly covered in pearls once again looks and feels like Heaven. The sounds of the bells ringing in the distance, calm water on the ponds, rainbows shimmer in places. The sounds of the laughter and the animals move about the countryside. Birds fly and do the butterflies and little sparks of light. But this time these are three figures walking down one of the golden streets. One of the figures is transparent, one is diaphanous, the third one walks on the golden street and with each step taken water splashes even though no water is evident on the street. Heaven is a very different place it seems now that the Fixer has been reborn here. It seems that these will be much to answer for soon. The Mako will be back to search for the hidden truths that live here too. These three must now decide the outcome of the discovery and the outcome of the demise of the Mako should the truth become aware to Hell itself. The Holy trinity must walk the streets of heaven and laydown the way to the truth then they must return to Hell and strike a covenant with Hell that the demise of the Mako will not prevent the fixer from fulfilling his position on the front line of the battle with the angles of Babylon. Man must not find Heaven and must not find Hell. Hell must not expose itself to man.

23/05/16 21:00

So, in the beginning the trinity is in play. Man has spread out across Asia, Europe, Africa, and throughout the Americas. Different religious have been set out and some of the originals have splintered. God moved Heaven far away from Earth so Man's power could not find it. Hell has always been sealed on an egg by god to keep it from spreading its hate and ebullience throughout the universe. In the beginning God buried truths on Hell, on Earth and on Heaven. They are the constant that keep everything in flux. Keeps everything fluid and maintains the constant push and pull of the cosmos. Man is moving out of the early days of the first metal forgeries. Powerful kingdoms are springing up everywhere on Earth. Early governments have little chance of holding on to power through as the God head leaders of the time cannot control land. Barons and their army's take of pillage plunder and slave trades. Man will eventually strike a civilization agreement with Land Barons. Thus, a way for God heads to control vast wealth and huge kingdoms. Hell, constantly sends messengers to earth to pull ant soul off the path of righteousness. Thus, the early death of Angels by luring anyone to riches instead of peace. Kill a protector Angel at the right time and a whole segment of people can suffer for hundreds of years due to loss of control of government and protector which may lead to slavery and certain damnation of vast numbers of souls. The plans are now in place for the coming storm man, science, progress the word of law and bureaucracy.

Heaven, Hell, and time. What do these things have in common? Well Heaven does have stars moving in regular synchronized movements which means a certain timing is applied to the environment of Heaven. Hell has an encasement surrounding it completely. However, as souls are amassed in the bowls of the River STYX, the whole mass of Hell pulses with life. This also suggest a rhythmic tide. Time, the breakdown is, a tide with a different termination, or ending, side of and extreme point. Now we know that time ends at the gate of Hell, also at the gate of Heaven. But now we know that timing is required to keep both Heaven and Hell with spirit. Spirit, this is how the truths are buried, the spirit in Hell yearns for salvation. The truth is buried under the River STYX and this is how the stripper takes the holy power from the soul to feed Hell. Thus, the soul is lost in Hell and lost in Heaven once stripped of its essence. The truth buried in Heaven is under the golden streets. This is the first place the soul comes into contact with Heaven as with the first step. The truth is in the meaning of gold itself. Ductile, malleable metal. The last is Guild, where all belong to the same class. The soul is drawn to the gold and stepping on to the streets becomes shaped into the heavenly body that perfectly matches all others. This I the promise of redemption. The gold of Heaven pays for all sins. The redeemer pays for all sins spiritually. The holy spirit continually replenishes, the gold for the redeemer as he walks on the streets and the Holy water splashes from his feet to cleanse all souls.

The souls in Heaven are saved, the souls in Hell are stripped. The souls on Earth are made at the time of conception. God then assigns an Angel and its protector to the new soul. The newborn babies either dies too early or lives a full life. The souls are either protected, trusted, promised to Heaven or Hell by an accompanying Heaven's Angel or Hells angel. The truth buried on Earth is to conceive itself. All is in this truth. To conceive is to have something from nothing. Hence the statement nothing is worth the cost. To conceive is to construct a soul, a soul comes from nothing to become everything that was. That is that will be. The fact that the Angels fly to and from Heaven or Hell and pass over Earth has no effect on the time nor does the effect of time on Earth affect the passing of angels. Hell sends Hellhounds and Demons to Earth to scare souls and people into making rash decisions. Heaven's Angels intercept these ill-fated grievances easily their armor alone will destroy a hell hound or fury demon. Hell needs souls and cannot always afford to send Hell's Angels to do battle, so distractions are needed. Heaven's Angels can fight as to always but lack a duality. The Christ has a duality but was not intended to fight, only absorb the sin of man. The fixer was designed to use his duality to mislead the redeemer thus limit the usefulness of Christ duality. As man becomes more powerful his arrogance and greed strip the power of the redeemer/Christ. Heaven's Angels lose the ability to protect man and his soul as the soul is misled.

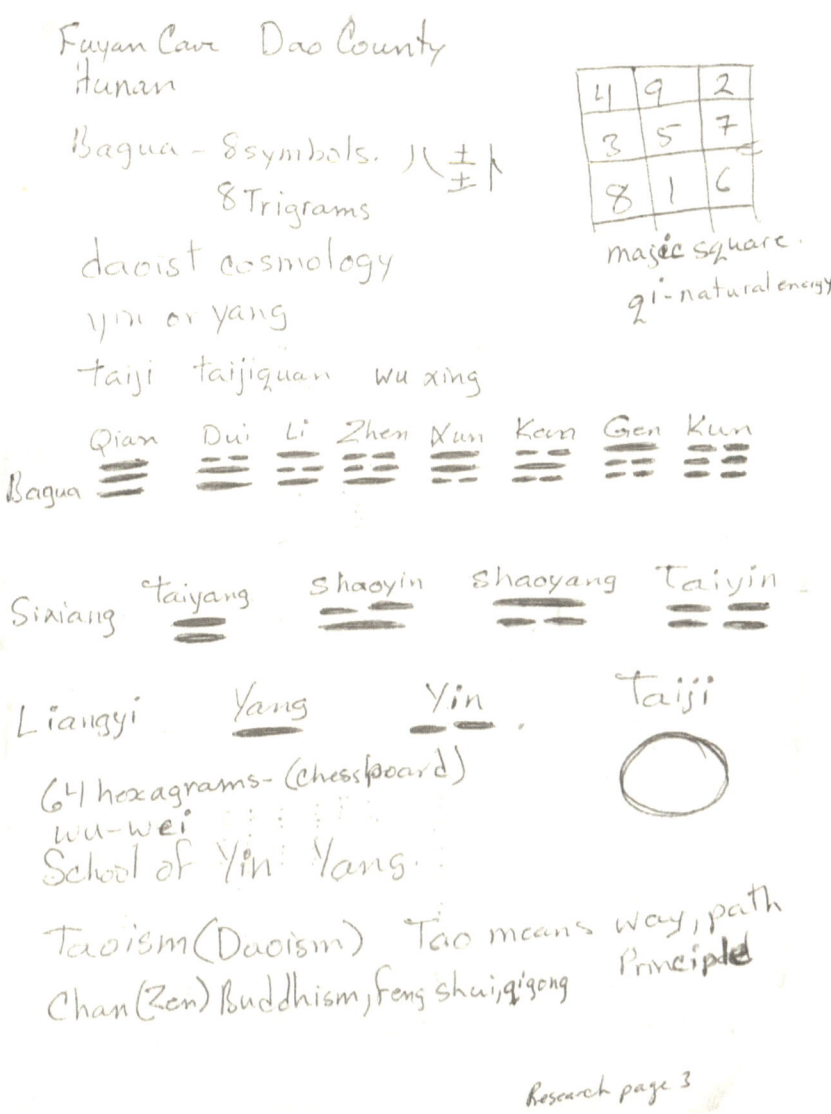

Fuyan Cave   Dao County
Hunan

Bagua – 8 symbols.)(± ℎ
         8 Trigrams   ±

daoist cosmology

yin or yang

taiji   taijiquan   wu xing

4 9 2
3 5 7
8 1 6

magic square.
qi – natural energy

Bagua
Qian Dui Li Zhen Xun Kan Gen Kun

Sixiang taiyang   Shaoyin   Shaoyang   Taiyin

Liangyi   Yang   Yin   Taiji

64 hexagrams - (chessboard)
wu-wei
School of Yin Yang

Taoism (Daoism) Tao means way, path
                                     Principle
Chan (Zen) Buddhism, Feng shui, qigong

Research page 3

24/05/16 22:30

Now we find man in the earlier days before recorded history. Metal forging is in its infancy, and water transport is limited to rivers, lakes and the Mediterranean Sea. Travel to and from the island of Japan out into the Indian Ocean. As well as travel back and forth across the

Bering Strait, Black sea, Red sea. Already at this time information gathering and trade routes are being established across the Atlantic Ocean by barges. The Atlantic trade route will grow to be strong soon, as the main political force is African women who control Africa as a whole from the eastern side of the continent. Later they would be called the Amazonian Kingdom. Travel by water across the smaller oceans is dangerous but the tonnage and the travelers is safe enough to establish a trade route. However, barges sent out on the tumultuous journey across the Atlantic is not fruitful. Barges in great numbers are lost to storms and get lost in the great many changing currents. Some do get through fewer still get back to the northwest of the African coast. Barges are set adrift from the Southern coast to be carried to hopefully the north coast of South America. The Barges are launched from the Central American area to be hopefully landed near what is to become Morocco. Many people who get across to the Americas stay and build up large colonies. Later as wealth builds both in the Americas and on North Eastern Africa, traded routs become strong as being able to somewhat control the barges with steers and early sails become useful and sea captains start to chart the stars route. This is the beginning of the cocaine, opium White and Red thin line.

The Thin red line, The Thin White line. Much later when man has gained control of the study of molecular composition and has the ability to study the cellular structure of any biological specimen with the use of an Electron microscope. He will find the evidence of cocaine in wide use in areas of Africa and the old Babylonian Empire. As well the use of opium and hasheesh in areas of South America and the Central Americas. Drugs have always been Mans best way of imagining possible religious routes to any God or demon. Some people gained an ability to control drug use to the point where reasons become real outcomes. The Soothsayer was borne. Contract with Angels were now possible, however not believable by the masses. And predictions fell short because of unforeseeable events leading to the death of the Soothsayer. This is the time of many conquests of armies in the Northern areas of Europe and Asia. Africa is very strong. The Babylonian is also very strong. The Magnolia and the Tibetan Shamanism is very much in control on the eastern side of the Himalayas. It is during this time that the Fixer and the Mako will come to the earth looking for truths buried by God as to the very nature of soul building. Early in prehistory man has not made the sound board, a very important discovery to understand the way sound transposes over and over a harp. Though to be the most beautiful sounding string instrument was offered to Angels in the early gilded cage. Man could not understand that sound needs to "bounce" to frame resonating waves. Which is what happens when you listen to your self-telling a story to someone.

In Heaven as in Hell, time is nonexistent. The Angels move back and forth between realms with no concern for life or the tides. Seasons on Earth are colorful changes in the lenses of the scenes. Souls from the future may be in Heaven at the same time as souls from the past. Souls in Heaven are not bound by time or the current that produces time, tides or the movement of the universe. The same is true of Hell. Souls are lost at an amazing rate at different times on earth. But Hell has no interest in a "when" you arrive to the River STYX. The only interest Hell has in a soul is the essence given off in passing through the Mako flew into Hell, avoided the Fixer's freeze because of the ghost of Hell in her head. She then surfed the STYX causing it to rise up and become ash on the banks of choke off the flow of the river. But the Mako did not find the truth beneath the. Hell used its Angels to remove the ash and the poisons river once again began to flow in its channel. Stripping the souls that cross over. Hell felt no pain and essentially lost no time due to the inconvenience made by the Mako. So the Mako and the fixer now make an appearance to Hell with a large number of other angels.

The entire crew shows up unannounced because of the Fixer's control of Hell's atmosphere. The reason is all the Heaven's angels Entourage. The Heaven's Angels may have been attacked when stepping out of their bubble by Hell. Hell has made no covenant with any heaven's angels ever. The Fixer will have his work cut out for him.

Hell has but one truth in it buried at the bottom of the STYX. Hell does not want any lost soul to find it nor any Hell's Angel. The possibility of a Mako here in the Hell is an unwanted occurrence and the Fixer will have to prepare for battle on a new and more scary scale before any such covenant is struck. Hell's Angels are flashing into the Hell one at a time from the formation in Heaven. The Fixer and his protector arrive with the others. Angels are not affected by place or time. They can move in and out of Hell, or to earth during any age on Earth and back to Hell or Heaven; like no time has passed in their respective homes. Time goes by on earth because of Man's free will. Time stops at both the gates of Hell and Heaven. The Fixer uses his duality to connect with the other Hell's Angels and freezes all Hell. The Heaven's Angels step out from their bubble to find Hell frozen, and so are they. The soon to be again Mako steps out directly in front of the Fixer just as planned. The Fixer looks into the eyes of his new protector. She looks into the eyes of the Hell itself. She feels the hate the pain the lost souls of Hell. She would be overwhelmed but for her wanting to the Mako again then for the second time her armor falls off. Again, she stands nude before the Fixer and all Hell, this time it will be different. This time there will be no going back to Heaven as a Heaven's Angel ever again. This time she will become the Mako forever and forever more the Mako will fly.

26/05/16 18:00

All Hell is frozen. Time is nonexistent, therefore; her body can't be burnt by Hell fire while her armor is off. The Fixer transplants the ghost of Hell into her conscience; it takes hold, and she is free again!

God's armor rises up and once again is clad on her body. This time the Holy water droplets are gone; the armor is now blackened by the hate of Hell. The lustrous shine is beautiful to see it truly is transcendence in fluid motion. God now reaches across the expanses and touches the Mako and her wings disappear, and this is replaced by the wings of Hell. Tears stream down her face from her eyes she is not Heaven's Angel anymore. He is not a Hell's Angel either. She truly is the Mako, she flies around Hell while it is frozen. Hell is furious at the Fixer and the Mako but is powerless to stop her and the Fixer. When Hell freezes over the Mako will fly to the STYX and discover its truth. The truth will set the Fixer free. Hell will fight the outcome of the truth. This will be a dangerous period for all Hell and Heaven will be included in this fight. Now the Mako once again surfs the STYX on her shield while holding her golden sword high. The STYX pours up ash on the banks the sight is awesome. The Mako is still crying she can hardly see for the first-time tears of Hate, fear, love, loss, discovery, pain, and joy are blurring her vision. The STYX is disemboweled to the banks, and the Mako discovers that Hell is actually hiding the truth of salvation beneath the STYX. The Mako then begins to replace the ash into the canal. The Mako instantly knows her fate.

A tearing at the atmosphere everywhere in Hell. The Fixer is bemused by the occurrence. What, more Heaven's Angels, A war! Here in Hell. What I can freeze them all! The Mako will have to make a decision, kill them all, or die instantly when I unfreeze all of them. Wait, this is different, what the fuck. Here! In Hell? They can't come here. Things are fucked for sure. I will have to unfreeze everyone and hope the confusion screws things up enough to get the Mako through a portal. The atmosphere splits everywhere. Heavens angels step out in an unconceivable number. The Trinity also has come. The transparent one, the diaphanous one, and the one who walks on water. Except no water here, not even Holy water is possible in Hell. As he takes every step on illumination is emitted and an ash drifts from his feet. They continue to walk to the banks of the River STYX and stop to look at the ash laden canal; then they stand and stare towards the Mako. Why aren't they frozen? What are they doing here? How can they come here in Hell? They are Holy personages. Here in Hell, can they still be Holy. The Mako flies to the Fixer and stands in his gaze.

She looks into his mind and the ghost of Hell talks to the Fixer. Your puzzled mind has the best of you Fixer. What the fuck did you think would happen. The Trinity cannot be frozen, nor can you freeze the Mako; they are all Dualities, and those three over there can tear this place to pieces whether you like it or not. Unfreeze everything, and may God be with you and the Mako.

Before the Mako can finish the last statement the diaphanous one flashes to be beside the Fixer and looks directly at the Mako. Peering into the Mako's duality, the Mako backs up slowly. The Mako speaks from the mind of God. Fixer, you will have to unfreeze everything. You cannot think an outcome of this and try to carry it out by surprise. We the Trinity can also freeze everything. We can also melt down Hell itself if necessary. We need you to keep your head, and your assaults to yourself. We have not come here to challenge you or your position. We have come here to align the Truth Child with Heaven. This child cannot understand the truths reasoning by simply exposing them one at a time. The truths have been laid down very carefully and more comprehensively than even a duality can perceive. The truth child will only spread fear amongst the Angels with the knowledge of the discovery. You release the Angels. I will freeze the Hell's Angels only. I will control the Heaven's Angels. I cannot freeze you or the Mako. If you flash with her, Hell will hunt you. Heaven will hunt you. I will hunt you down and destroy the Mako before you. You must make good your destiny to be on the front line at the battle of Evermore. You will be there, even if we must replace you with another. The duality of him reveals he is God. The Fixer knows he has more respect for God than any of the Trinity and unfreezes Hell. Instantly I cannot look onto the light of God. I the Fixer, am rendered powerless in Hell. The transparent one is the Holy Spirit, disappears into all the Heaven's Angels. Hell is on fire.

The Hell's Angels are frozen, the Heaven's Angels are held by the Holy Spirit. The Christ is now beside the Fixer. They two cannot connect; the Fixer was created to destroy the Christ. The Christ was designed to absorb the sins of man and save the souls so they would not arrive here. The Mako is out of control of Heaven and Hell. God is impossible to look upon. The brilliance of light is spend out from appoint to everywhere in Hell. Still God is moving separately from the light source, God will control Hell and the Fixer will be saved by the grace of God. The Mako is the only duality that cannot be controlled and must decide to remain the protector of the Fixer or run to the world and bring only pain to man and run to Heaven. As the Mako can only know what has and is. What will is not me. I am seeking only truth, the Ghost of Hell from inside. Hell can't control the Hell Ghost while it is in my conscience; God can't control it either I need the truth to fulfill my destiny; however the Fixer cannot lust after the truth knowing God saved him in Heaven. I am with the Fixer; the truth will wait in Heaven and on Earth. Fixer I am with you, I am on your side. Fixer come to me we will stand together, we will be, Hell cannot allow God to hold sway we must return to Heaven to do Gods bidding and I will be at your side always. Heaven's Angels begin to step into a portal. We flash and are gone to Heaven; God is alone in Hell. God lifts the controlling power Hell is on fire, God is light.

28/05/16 23:00

God, I have a covenant with you, you cannot break it. If you break this covenant, Heaven and Hell will start to break down. Your precious man will stop providing souls. You and I will starve; time will leak into our exile and consume us. I am Hell you cannot break your covenant with me. I will hurt this Mako and the Fixer to the death and I plan to replace the Fixer with one that is terribly bad. I want the Mako, you must deliver the Mako tome. The River STYX will be fixed easy enough but the Mako has my ghost of Hell in her, I want it back and the Mako is to die where it started, on the banks of the STYX. God, I am Hell, hear me I will not stop until I have what I want, no matter what the cost is. I am light, I am, I will, I promise, I protect every soul that man makes. Even if I am delivering that soul to Hell. That is the covenant I have with you. I am, that is all that is needed to be on you seeking breath. I will, you can count on that. I promise every promise made by me is fulfilled. I protect even your soul, I protect the soul of Hell and it lives in the STYX. I command thee Hell, I am God your Lord, I command thee Hell you will not entrust your lord, or I will bring about your end by thine on hand here and now at whatever the cost. The truth child is necessary discovered the Fixer will be set free. Hell will hunt the Mako I will promise, trust and protect the Mako to the gates of Hell. You will have your revenge, the battle of evermore will have its Fixer.

Hellfire is the worst thing a soul can imagine. Souls that are being exposed to a Hell on fire as the rage moves about and back and forth up and down the STYX. The canal must begin to flow again, I will have the essence of God running through me again. I am Hell; I will have my taste of Heaven. I will have my Angels take Hell to the Earth. I will take Hell to Heaven and I will have my revenge on the Mako. I will extract another phantom from the STYX. I will use it to draw out the Mako, and if I can, I will destroy the Fixer and replace it with a fucking Angel that doesn't get to feel anything. A duality that fucks things up on Earth and in Heaven is what I'm planning. God commands me I will obey, I will because I am Hell. Go ahead Fixer; knock on Hell's gate I've been waiting. The brightest light Hell has even seen is beginning to fade as God quits shedding his light and leaves Hell. God doesn't require a portal. God is lights, god is in everything and is everywhere at the same time. God moves about the universe without effort or need for transport. Hell doesn't even truly understand this. God's truth is undeniable in the universe and needs no courage. God flashes as light and our spirit move with grace throughout everything everywhere and finally arrives at the *Gates of Heaven* itself. Everything about Heaven is now of a pearl as when the Mako released the portal of saltwater on the street of Heaven and pearls poured out from the Heavens. What a beautiful sight and the Gates of Heaven, Pearl Nautilus.

The Pearl Nautilus, the Gates of Heaven are after portside of the Pearl Nautilus. This vessel is captained by Nemo, The Spirit and breath of God. God is in everything everywhere and now in Heaven is the Pearl Nautilus. Heaven's Angels in a number too, great to count portal into Heaven. They disappear as fast as they emerge into Heaven to become as wind gently blowing or light passing, and the sounds of bells running in the distance. The Fixer flashes into Heaven along with the Mako. The Fixer and the Mako make their way down a golden street; the Mako is now not allowed to touch the street just as the Fixer cannot. The soul burns in the head of the Fixer and the Mako has a ghost of Hell in her Head. Every step they take is just above the street and smoke drifts from their feet. The street heals itself behind them. God has prepared the way they must walk in Heaven. The Mako has a protector Angel with her. The Fixer has a Hell's Angel and its protector with him. The way has been set; the path they must take will bring them past and under the Helm of the Nautilus. The group of six stop on the street directly below the Helm and this is the crossroad in Heaven. Now the Trinity walks toward them from out of nowhere in front of them. To their left and right souls run, jump and dance. Lights bounces in the air butterflies and birds dart all around. The Trinity stop the diaphanous one speaks. I am your God. I am the one that has breathed life into all souls in heaven and hell. I have brought you to the crossroads in Heaven.

There is this reason I brought you to the crossroads. I now charge the Mako that she discovers the truth buried here. This is how the Fixer will be set free from the discourage. The Mako found in hell the two combined truths will be freedom the Fixer requires. The Mako rises up slowly and gases downward to the group of four looking towards the Trinity, the crossroads of Heaven, looking to the left is the starboard to the right is the port in front is the stern and behind is the bow. The four directions in Heaven are Entrance, Loyalty, Orientation, Mission. The truth of the crossroads is Will. One who enters must be loyal, orient and conduct their mission here in heaven. God's Will, will be done in Heaven. The truth of Salvation in Hell is buried under the STYX because it is the tripper of the souls. The essence is Gods will and the true power of God. When you first reach the crossroads, you must have Gods Will go in any direction in Heaven or on Earth. This is the truth of the crossroads anywhere it is Universal; therefore, the Fixer must be set free. I descend slowly and stand before the Fixer. I speak Fixer not the Ghost of Hell. I have made the discovery of the truth of the crossroads. Together with the truth I discovered in Hell under the STYX; I now release thee from the bondage of Hell. I tell thee that Salvation is what you seek and here at the crossroads, where you find your will to go in any direction in the universe. Your will sets you free Fixer Salvation is not possible without the will to take your direction.

The Fixer is motionless, the Christ now walks past us, and down the road behind us. Water splashes up on us as he passes beads stick to me here, and there, and to my Heaven's Angel. Where they land on the Fixer and the other Hell's Angels flashes of light scatter. The Christ walks in the direction of mission. The Diaphanous one turns right and walks toward orientation. The Transparent one turns around and walks toward Loyalty. The Transparent one says to the Fixer as he leaves "Choose wisely, your direction here and your Will, will lead you to your Salvation." Then without notice there appears two pairs of wings floating in midair above the crossroads. The Mako turns to look at them. They are beautiful, the Fixer rises above the crossroads and announces, "I Will, that I walk with the Holy Spirit, I will follow him." There is a bright flash of light from the crossroad. The Fixer and Mako are transfixed as their wings fall off and disappear into the Golden Street and the Heaven's wings, takes their place on their backs. God speaks these things that are done at the crossroad can never be taken back, for now you must walk the road to your destiny. Salvation lies in your loyalty to each other. The Mako is even now being hunted by Hell. Hell will never stop until it has its revenge, that is the true hate that burns in Hellfire, "Revenge". Fixer you must be loyal to the Mako if she is to discover the other truths. The Mako must die at the hands of Hell on the Banks of the STYX. Fixer you must avenge the Death of the Mako at the front line of Evermore.

29/05/16 22:30

I am here! Mako do you remember my Will? Mako, I am here at the front line of Evermore! When first you fought me, I froze you, I put the Ghost of Hell in you. Your armor fell off. I left you alone in heaven, your nude body: so beautiful made of milk and honey. Mako, I am looking directly at one of your sisters now. She looks a lot like you. She is beautiful, her armor is deadly to me, but she is frozen like you were, and soon her armor will fall like most of all the Heaven's Angels here. God is in everything, he is everywhere. The Holy Spirit is here too, Hell is here, because I am here. Below us the Earth is older than us. The Earth has changed with the advance of Man. Man fell prey to science and politics. I count 25000 years since the Mako was first contrived by the Ghost of Hell. How do these people justify their existence? They hate each other they make debts and build empires. Their offspring then break the bonds that hold the empires together and war breaks out millions die needlessly. Souls are gathered by Hell's Angels in droves and driven straight to Hell. Hell has made many gains from the souls of man in the last years. Now Hell feels with the Mako taken at the banks of the STYX; that it surely has the power to break the Trinity. Here at the evermore, Babylon and its Angels are here. The Mahdi has arrived; the *Al-Masih-Dajjal* is among us. Also, *Armillas, Eschaton* has come with *Kalki, Maitreya*, The *Samuel Tannin* or *Tunannu*, and *Hybris*. The Four Horse Men have ridden out across the Earth, and war is everywhere! The air is insipid, the ground is barren, and the water is tainted.

30/05/16 23:00

I hang in the air, motionless; my blackened charred body is grotesque, burnt by the fires of Hell. The look of me is muscular, large powerful chest, a spine that stands out on my back. Legs like that of a powerful horse. But end in long clawed feet instead of a hoof. Arms are long, powerful, heavily boned, and end also in clawed hands. My face looks like that of a tiger, only completely burnt to the bone. Only the armor of burnt flesh is left on the bones of the face. There are no eyelids. The eyes are of blackest coal and have a shine of the dead. The vapor that pours out all around the eye opening is the result of the Hellfire on the coal, and the mixture of the souls that burn in my head. The essence leaks out and continuously supplies the vapor. I look, feel, taste, and smell like Hell. On my back are the wings that God gave me thousands of years ago when the Mako stood at my side at the crossroads in Heaven. The wings do not even look more than minutes old. But they have carried me through so much since first they came to me. I look around without moving. The sky is full of Angels, Heaven's Angels and Hell's Angels; Too numerous to count, too numerous to even grasp in a duality. God and Hell have put everything into this final battle. God has promised to completely destroy Hell by throwing down every star in Heaven, straight at Hell to obliterate it from any place it may hide. Hell has promised to destroy every Heaven's Angel and then attack the Pearl Nautilus with everything it has left all the grains of sand in all the beaches of the Earth. We are all just grains of sand. I will, promise trust and protect, the ebb of the tide has just exposed us at the end.

02/06/16 23:30

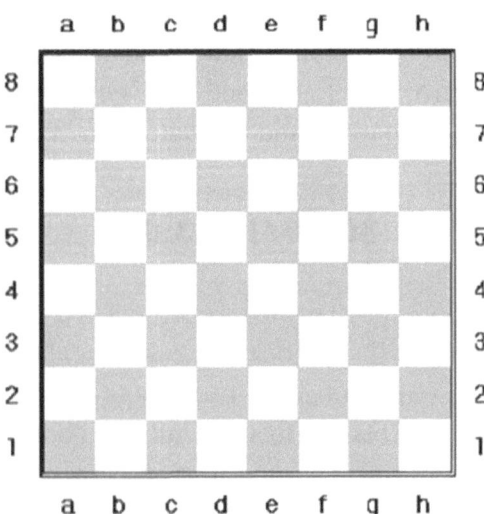

Hell's Angels flash in to view, Heaven's Angels portal and stop from their bubbles. The Fixer and the Mako step out of portals. These are the Six. The Mako must find truth on Earth and she will start here in the Himalayan area of Southern Asia. The Great Mountains are home to one of the future seers *"The Tibetan Empire"*. Buddhist Monks, Spiritual leaders with a special ability to visualize future events and variation of each of powerful stimulants, *opium. Hasheesh* and now; but rare and only available in limited supply cocaine. And the use of a newly discovered game that we call chess, in the modern world. Called in Aristotle's time *Latruncularius*. During the great African empire, *"Skaak"* and in area of the Chinese lands, *"棋"*. The game plays on a board of 64 evenly sized squares of opposite colors, a duality. The board is marked with numbers 1-8 on each side and letters of the language a-h. You will notice the board starts with

The number 1 at each end of play. This means that 1 is 8 and 2 is 7, 3 is 6 And so on. One field of play overlaps the other another duality. The game has 16 pieces or figures on each side in the first two rows of squares. The back rank is an elephant, spear man, angel, soothe seer, God head, Angel spearman, elephant. The second rows of eight are all trained fighting monks. These pieces are placed on both sides of the board in order. The right-hand corner of the board must be a white square with the God head on its opposite color and the soothe seer on its color. The pieces move one player turn each, and each piece has a specific type of movement by using the letters and unmarks on the board, a location on the board can become a historical location and the entire game can then be historical fact, for the use of study. Thus a way to analyze each outcome and future outcomes analyzed by setting a time limit on each game a player sees the mortality in each piece, thus giving the game "Life" and the fighting monks become the souls on a game board handled by a player in a game struck by time. Trying to find one outcome at a time, the forces at play on the board become transcendent and allow the mind to combine thought and movement by opposing consciousness in each of the two players. Allowing each player once skilled to experience a sense of duality and doing so on a powerful drug; the mind is able to imagine himself a duality even if only during the time the drug affects the conscience and while struggling against the forces in play.

12/06/16 22:30

Now, the Mako is a powerful being because, this is the land of transcendence and the time is that of transposition. Vast numbers of people are working the land in large, luscious valley areas. Thus, providing huge food quotas that support large armies and for the first time in Man's history of education is being practiced among large number of wealthy people. Some are removing themselves to isolated places high in the mountain of the Himalayas. These people begin to practice sensory deprivation. All the while communing in groups high above in fortress clinging to the mountain headlands. Generations go by and record keeping begins, rudimentary at first and insight is slow but with the use of trained scribes, history taking begins. Followed by scholarship, sect and secularism; Priest hoods, devotions, meditation, yield long string theory devotees. They produce skilled deliberators, able to follow a particular path of thought on one skill over several generations. Along with the historical material scholar of any doctrine, can reasonable conclude out comes of many personal experiences with good results. Once these theoretical lines of thought are analyzed by scholar of the time, they begin to realize the need for a way to utilize dualities of reasoning and along with the use of drug induced sensory deprivation. The most skilled of each sect decide to have contests of physical prowess and mental conditioning. It's at this time the game chess or *skaak* is born and leads to the first future seers better known as *Prophets*.

The group of Six will move amongst these people of devotion and look for any sign of truths. Hell will hunt them anywhere, that includes this place. I fly over vast expanses of what will be *Xizang Zizhiqu*. These are the days of *Nuwa & Fuxi*, the Mako is with me as well as our four protector angels. The Mako has told us to fly in the direction of Kunlun Mountains. The *Tarim Pendi*, dry and land. It's of no matter to us, the people here can't see us fly, I dive down to skim the surface of the land, as I gaze around, I feel Hell. I smell Hell; I look up to the group. Two of them are drifting smoke- the Hell's Angels, the other three don't. I do, my burnt body still smokes as I fly. I see two more smoke trails behind the group I flash, I briefly pass through Hell, Holy Fuck! I've never seen so many Hell's Angels and a huge gathering of Hellhounds, demons and furies, I flash. I appear in front of the two trailing the group I freeze them. I want the truth this time. I'm not the Mako; I look into the burning souls of these two fucking things. They know they are about to die for real this time. I get the message loud and clear. I unfreeze them; I wave them to follow me and we are on the group in seconds. I scream and howl the group stops. I quickly enlighten them. We are about to be attacked, these two have been sent by God, not Hell. They will exchange wings with us so we can better hide during the battle. The smell of Hell is all around us here on Earth, I look down and the ground seems to be moving with demons.

The Hell's Angels fly to be beside the Mako and the Fixer. Flashes of light and a large pull on the atmosphere bubbles and Portals everywhere, the Mako and the Fixer exchange wings with the Hells Angels. Holy Shit! They are here; the Trinity has come along with more Heaven's Angels, the sky is illuminated by the presence of God, The Holy Spirit and The Christ. There are new streaks of light and smoke coming from the East and the west sides of China. The whole sky is alive with spirits and dragons. There is something different happening, it appears as though our presence has not gone unnoticed by scouts of the Spirit of Eurasian Deities. Jesus, Hades and Poseidon. Indra, Yama and Varuna Yahweh. The Babylonian Angels, and that smell. The smell of hallucinogens, such as opium, hasheesh, cannabis, and poisonous toxins coming from fire burning on mountains, and from Fungi burning. There are large sea serpents swimming up the swollen river. I see a large turtle and all the monsters from Hell running along the ground, some of them can fly, and there are colors drifting in the air; these are gas clouds used to feed the virtual demons, as well as to strike fear in the hearts of the Angels of God. Man will see these days of war in the Heavens as, meteor showers, extreme amounts of rain. Lightning bolts of unimaginable frequency. Volcanoes will erupt, the Earth will shake and split-up Heaven and Land, and Mountains will crumble. Meteors will strike the land and streak across the sky, fires will burn, and toxic gasses will escape the Earth, the oceans will wash up all manner of beasts from deep under the sea on the beaches. Huge whales, squid, sharks, tornados will literally throw fish all over the land. and toss livestock for miles into lakes and oceans. Hurricanes will blow from the ocean to the land causing tidal waves to flood vast areas with saltwater. This will change the bays and inlets, wipe out cities, fishing, farms and annihilate small civilizations as well as species of animals already stressed, and plants. Whole forests burn, rivers change course, lakes dry up. Desserts appear where grasslands where areas remain flooded for decades, mass starvations of animals and humans. The sky blackens with birds of all types and insects, huge migrations of animals traverse the land trying to escape floods, fires, smoke toxic plumes, and so this is why it smells like Hell on Earth, howling, burning flesh, poisonous gases, breaking bones, screams suffering of people and livestock. The sky is continually changing colors and it is very hard to tell what time of day it is as celestial bodies not seen before travel across the sky. Lighting the night sky like daytime, and blocking the sunshine at times. All of the Gods have come to pay homage to the Mako, the Mako is named in older languages on Earth, some these are; , Kindvandie Waarheid, 真理之子, Anak ng Katotohanan, Đứa con của sự thật, Дитя истины, το αληθινό παιδί του Θεού, 진실의 아들, ਸੱਚ ਦਾ ਬੱਚਾ, सत्य का बच्चा.

The different religious people were terrified by the loss of life, the volcanoes, flowing lava, the fire storms, streaks of light in the skies, great floods and sea life found on dry land. The Gods are fulfilling a prophecy foretold by the Goddesses of the People of Prehistory. Mankind used to worship Goddesses. The reign of these deities started when man started tool building and lifted in a small group of 30-500 persons. The Goddess helped childbirth and Animal Husbandry and started crop sharing. This lasted till large civilizations grew in areas of Africa, Asia minor, East Asia, and India. During and before the Sanskrit, Vedic Sanskrit with the early trade route across the Atlantic by barge. Trade in food stuffs, Hallucinogenic drugs, people, some animals and religious ideology. Areas including South America, central and southern areas of North America were part of the Goddess Deities areas of worship. The Goddess' Deities prophesied their replacement with Gods and Demons, as societies grow more war like and less propitiatory, and the last of the great Goddess civilization died with the Greek Trojan war. Where the Amazonian women warriors were at their strongest were over reached by their joining forces with the Greeks to destroy the Trojans, The Great Addas Ababa fell to invading warriors from the East as large numbers of Amazon warriors were in battle in and around the Mediterranean. The home warriors were outnumbered and the whole Goddess Nation that composed of *Africa* including *Egypt, Saudi Arabia, Iraq, Jordan, Syria, Jerusalem* was annihilated.

And now we fly amongst monsters, beasts, Gods, Demons, Dragons and the Child of Truth fly's as the Mako through the mayhem of Gods and Demons striking out at each other while the Earth is being tested by forces from the great species above and beyond its location in orbit. The Gods and Goddesses are changing places and the Earth is being assaulted from the heavens and changes from under the surface of the continents. We fly unhindered by the changes going on and on the Earth. The people that are moving on the Earth do not see us or all that have gathered to witness the flight of the Mako. The struggle of man is not our concern only that some of the very highly trained persons may view our passing through drug induced visions, or Shamanistic practices of perception. Stories will travel the Globe of the Sky demons and Dragons huge turtles and what looks like Cities of Light floating in the sky. Leading whole groups of God worshiping people to try many ways to ascend to the Heavens, some try to fly, some travel to mountain tops, some build tall towers and a very few try build a stairway to heaven. All the Gods including Buddha, Allah, Jehovah, the Twelve Olympians, Zeus, Hara, Poseidon, Demeter, Athena, Apollo, Artemis, Ares, Aphrodite, Hephaestus, Hermes, Dionysus. Their parents Cronus and Rhea have cities of light in the sky and stairways are the way of mankind to them, Both in the legend and in spirituality. So, the Gods welcome mankind's pursuit to ascend Heavens staircase.

13/06/16 23:00

I am the Fixer; I fly with the Mako we now have the wings of Hell upon our backs again. It feels right to have these wings back Heaven's wings are awesome but lack allure of flash with my **Hellish** personality. The Mako looks awesome dressed in Hell's wings, she is fucking beautiful, blackened armor, blackened wings, skin of milk, long golden hair, blue diamonds. I want to fuck her as we fly over the Hell that is everywhere below us and all around the Mako only has eyes for the truth, the ghost of hell in hear head will want to get fucked. What the fuck lets fly to the Kunlun Mountains and find something to make her trip her success. Hell has found the space between us and Earth to be the only room for it to move on us. The sky everywhere is full of flying beast and dragons, Heaven's Angels and Gods from the far reaches of the universe. Hell has no power to fight these deities. Hell will have to wait fuck you Hell, fuck you I fly down and up demons and hell hounds apart for shits and giggles. I fly straight at Hell's Angels and cut some to shreds some fight back fuck you I want to kill all of you, I'm the Fixer. I scream to the Mako get down in here fuck these things up now, she flies down the Ghost of Hell has taken a liking to the chance to kill some of the things and maybe something else. The Mako spins, twists and flashes appears and disappears. Demons and dragons, Hellhounds and Heaven's Angels shredded she screams as she sends her sword through a Heaven's Angel and a Hell's Angel. Then surfs The Shyok River on her shield, *"The River of Death"*. We have flown out of Tibet and entered India; however, in the times we fly, these countries are not established yet. The people are different in language and teaching, but God head government leaders are war like, and large civilizations do not exist yet. Surfing the river on her shield is an excellent way to chase these monsters. Some chase the Mako. I dive into the River and move under the surface; we move as a group. The group of eight Immortals Towards the Hindu Kush and the Old Khmer. Also, what is now called *Uttar Pradesh*. As we move to the Uttar Pradesh the River Ganges & Yamuna run together at the Allahabad and the Ganges flows East. Towards the Kunlun we see the lavish paradisiacal details beauty; with gem like rocks, cliffs towering made of Jade and Jasper. Plants are exotic and bejeweled, the Lake of Gems lays at the base of the mountains Deities such as *Xi Wangmu, Yushi, Tai di*, and *Sun Wukong* have made this place home. The mountains have seemingly Golden Ramparts and Roman Angel look like a huge castle covered in Gemstones and bejeweled plants. Sanskrit called *Sailaraja*- The king of the mountains. This is what we will be called, but now the Mako is seeking the truth buried here in the *Kunlun, Hindu Kush, Caucasus Indicus* and the western *Himalayas* Region.

28/06/16 22:00

The Hellish beast drop away from us as we travel upriver to the Lake of Jewels.

ਗਹਿਣਿਆਂ ਦੀ ਝੀਲ

நகைகளின் ஏரி

The water surface is calm and smooth. I move just below the surface will out disturbing the water, the group of the Angels above us move across the lake and break apart only as we reach the Eastern edge of shoreline. There are several huge headlands jutting out over the water, giving the cliffs and mountainous areas a hallucinatory dream quality. We eight stand on a rocky shoreline and gaze upwards to the out cropping's of *"Jade & Jasper"* cliffs, and the buttresses of rock that support overhanging projections over promontory's that jut out into the water. The Mako looks everywhere then flies to many of the outcropping and sits still as if waiting for someone to advance on our position. Looking out across the water, I notice we have company Dragons and Angels are flying towards us. Then I see Cities of Light hanging in the distant sky all manner of beasts of the water are moving beneath the surface. Also, a gathering of mortals to the North of our position. There are 10's of thousands of people in the front are religious leaders and royalty. They are of different cultures from *Punjabi, Japanese, Chinese, Arab, African, and Greek*; they are *Buddhist, Hindu, Amazonians, Muslim, Shinto, many people speak in Vedic Sanskri*t. The language is beautiful to listen to and they are singing it to us some of the drug induced Shamans can see us, so sing.

The *Uttarakhand*, Land of Gods, the truth that the Mako seeks is before us now. The people that are making the long perilous trek up the S*hyok River*, thought country that has been changing rapidly with the coming of the God these people are not alone, more than 50 thousand have come along with their Angels. It is truly a sight to see hundreds of thousands of Angels fly all around these people, above and below the earth. Along with some of their deities I fly up to be with the Mako, I see why she is watching from this vantage. The water is shimmering from fires burning all along the distant shoreline. The sky is filled with colors, in the far distance a volcano is filling the sky with a fiery glow that pulses with convection. I am the Mako, I have come here for the truth that has to be started here and now. I flash to the group. I motion to the two Hell's Angels with wings from God with a force known only by the ghost in my head the two give up their wings immediately. The fixer follows suit. The Angels of Hell look amazing as they continuously emit trails of smoke and the blushes mist from their eyes. I fly across the lake and become immersed in humanity they can't see me as I move amongst them. Then I come to a group of people who are setting up a kind of hospital mostly for pregnant women and those with broken bones. I look around me; the group of eight is here. I look to the Fixer; his duality is admonished with my intent. I am the Mako and the truth is here and now! Angels from heaven begin to chant and then I ask them to provide me their shields. I hand shields to the group of eight

The Angels of Hell have never handed a shield before, things in Heaven are not in the realm of Hell. I fly above the ground; I hold my shield up and then I strike it with my sword. The shield immediately explodes as the portal is destroyed the lightning bolt streaks out in all directions as the portal passed its power to me. The salt water in the shield is vaporized by the lightning bolt sword and the resulting steam is minute particles of Holy water that drifts down upon the group of eight. They are holding the shields above their heads so as to be protected from the Holy water but not completely, I settle beside them. The holy water makes us visible to humanity. People fall to their knees, some stand and chant some sing and move in rhythmic dance. The crowd splits from many different places. The Shamanistic leaders move through the breaks in the crowd. They are beautiful, graceful and confident. They all are carrying a flower and a piece of fruit; they are peach blossoms and fruit is golden peach. The religious leaders want to commune with us and offer their blossoms and fruit for our approval. I take the flowers and walk through the pregnant childbearing woman and give them the blossoms, then I strike the ground and plant a seed from a peach. This tree will grow to be thousands of years old, and will provide a fruit approximately every 6000 years that will give a mortal, immortality. That a group of thinkers and religious people may flourish in this region to have constant contact with the Gods and Deities. People here will call the Peach Festival, and immortality will be possible.

03/07/16 23:00

I watch the Mako as she strokes the ground and plants the peach seed. Unbelievably she starts to flicker her blackened armor becomes translucent, and then blackened then translucent. The wings of Heaven flash as if they are wings of hell. The Mako flashes and the Ghost of Hell in her is all that is visible. The Hellish thing is also beautiful, fucking awesome. Gods armor falls to the ground all around the Ghost of Hell. Suddenly the ground begins to shift in place and the Diaphanous one appears. The brilliant light is striking as the mist of Holy-Water continues to fall, into this the most holy of all. God speaks through the Fixer to the Mako. This truth you are seeking here is the most dangerous. You have an unbelievable ability to extract truths. I am powerless to stop you from this discovery; however, this truth seals your fate with Hell. I know that all we see is the Ghost of Hell, but I also know that the Mako is Between Gates now and can hear what this ghost hears Mako, uncover this truth do not let the Ghost of Hell do this, the power of the Truth. Child is more confident than this beast. The Ghost of Hell spreads the wings of heaven screams and the Holy water spills on the beast, a Hellfire breaks out and the beast is consumed as a blueish fog lifts from her. The armor begins to shimmer and glow, then it is translucent and finally changes to its original beauty, pure white, white as snow on a frost covered mountain. Then more flashes as the Ghost of Hell burns completely from Hell Fire and the Mako returns to her wings. Her beautiful body is completely naked before us all. Then the armor, gods pure love lifts and is again on her. This Angel of Heaven is now one with immortality.

The Ghost of Hell is now gone to once again be with Hell. The Mako is now a new Angel. The Truth Child is now with her because of this discovery and the sealed fate by God and his covenant with Hell. The light dims and the Diaphanous one is gone. I look upon the Mako she looks just as she did when first I laid eyes on her and froze her. Beautifully, strong, confident, and now a duality with a holy spirit in her, not a Ghost of Hell. Mako, what is the truth, what have you come here for? To plant a seed for mortals to dream of immortality. Have you come here to give new life a dream to cling onto the Truth Child? The Mako walks around the glides toward me. She is not walking on this earth she is not here for us or them. The truth is not apparent to anyone but her. The Truth Child and God. She bends down and reaches out and pulls a sword a lightning and a portal of saltwater from nowhere. She is an Angel of God once more. Fixer I am not of your realm anymore. I am a Heaven's Angel again; I came here to discover a truth. Fixer you have come to here to be set free. I will show you the truth, the truth will set you free. I will be here with your council for some time as you explore your freedom. Whether we are once again together will depend on you and your actions. I must take refuge here amongst these people and assist their assent to and from various Gods and deities, as well as the Cities of Light and while the demons roam the blood soaked battle fields, amidst the chaos of the Gods & goddesses exchanging roles. Are you ready, Fixer are you ready, Are you ready, for your freedom?

The Fixer flashes his wings, screams and howls. I am ready for anything; I am the Fixer! I have come here to be with you, to find the truth. I have come here to be with the immortals, The gods of the earth. I have come here to correct mistakes of old. What truth have you that sets me free? What truth have you found here at the start of the peach festival, the immortal ground that we stand upon? The Mako, in a grand gesture with her sword above her head points in all the directions as she speaks. This land, the land of the Gods. This land will keep the truth of immortality safe for thousands of years till the End of Days on Earth. This land will change one mortal every 6000 years into an immortal through the Peach festival and the elixir derived by some shamanistic medicine men and his concubine as for told by the immortals here. These immortals will need to replenish their immortality every 3000 years by returning here to drink the elixir. Some of these immortals will create beasts and demons on earth through their misdeeds and chance meetings with the ghost of Hell that once was in me, and now resides in a city far off to the West of here called, Babylon. Fixer, the truth here is not the immortality to certain individuals or the practice of the Peach festival in this land, but the immorality of God himself. After I planted the seed, I left this place, I stood between the gates of Heaven and the Hell and watched the Ghost of Hell change my body. And I was able to understand how immortality works. The souls are created here on earth and go through a series of trials. Some of these souls never leave the womb. Some have children some are barren, God needs these souls to be immortal, and so does Hell.

But the immortal is a creation of God and not Hell. Fixer you are an immortal, a creation of God not Hell, you were trapped in Hell, part of a Great Test by both Heaven & Hell. Only, you used your power to heal and save a soul and to free yourself. God gave you that power. Once freed, you became a rouge force that challenges The Christ. You then created me. I am the Mako, only envisioned by God himself as a possibility of your freedom from Hell. Now your freedom from serving the Mako will be the reason I must now take refuge here on Earth. Fixer the Earth is like a tree, the seeds of souls are a testing ground for the immortality of Gods and deities. They can be cloned or expanded at the same time, this way immortals can never challenge the Gods as they have a constant source of essence while the immortals cannot be cloned or reproduce, and their essence is not transferable. It was through your great test in chains, in a cell locked away in Hell that God was able to trace a soul's essence through the mortal by testing clones of the ones sent on by you. Once freed, God then needed to create the Christ. And now you are free to challenge all the coming gods and the duality Christ when he arrives on Earth. Fixer, You and I were reborn in Heaven, we traveled to Hell where I slough through the River STYX. I separated the dead lost souls from their essence and peeled off the poisonous river and exposed the truth there. Then we were at the crossroads in Heaven where the truth there was your own Will, and the freedom that it brought you here. Now you can test your own immortality, chase that Ghost in Hell and challenge any duality that may confront you. I wish you god speed and I wish to see you again at my side before I die on the banks of STYX.

I am an Angel of Hell; I have been reborn in Heaven. I have stood at the crossroads in Heaven. I have been hunted by Hell and its demons. I am now in the land of the Gods with the Mako as she now assumes her role as a duality without the Ghost of Hell. I fly at her and scream. She stands motionless, I look into her eyes, she looks into mine. I feel her duality it is much stronger than previously. I walk around her and through the group of eight. I stop at one of the two who followed us. I exchange wings with him. I dawn heavens wings once more they were given to me at the crossroads in heaven when I received free will. I will wear them till time on Earth stops. I flash, I remerged over the lake or jewels. I flash I reemerge over Babylon; several Angels rise from the portal under the city straight from Hell. They start to fly in circles around me. This is going to be an exercise in pure justice. They flash I flash I move between the gates of Heaven and Hell I reemerge where they were. They are now where I was waiting for my return. They are more than a little angry and intend to change my position with Hell. I freeze them. I look into their minds. They are mostly vacant beings except the Ghost of Hell that was in the Mako. I hold them in a frozen sate until the Angels are all on fire. Hellfire surrounds the group. I can kill them all here and now. Hell can't stop me these things are not capable of putting up a fight against me. I cause the Ghost to transplant into me once again where she was before I planted her into the Mako I then steal one more ghost. I unfreeze the group there are six of them, 4of them drift down. I fly and kill one of the vacant Angels. That's right go to Hell.

I turn to the other vacant Angel she is still on fire; I grab her and flash. We are in Hell. Hell moves a group of Angels and beasts towards us as we arrive. I freeze all of them; the vacant Angel is no longer on fire and is healing as I plant two ghosts of Hell in her head. I look at her and I study the new duality, I let her see my duality, my pain my great test and the final escape and how Hell and Heaven hunted me. I am losing my group on her as her duality begins to take hold and her conscious possess her new power: She breaks free and flies around Hell screaming and slashing at demons and beasts of Hell. Then she flies to me and reaches out. I hand her the sword I hold and the shield as well. We know instantly and we flash. We reemerge in a place where I once was, when I stood on the shores of the Lake of Jewels with the Mako. Everyone is gone the people, the Gods, the Dragons and Cities of Light. The place doesn't look the same either. It appears as though much time has passed by while I have been away in Hell. We must find the Mako, we must find the group of Eight. The Mako does not have to die on the shore of the STYK The Earth can have its final battle, but I must change the outcome for Heaven and Hell with this new duality. The truths that are found can swing the balance in favor of Heaven. The stars can continue to shine on in the universe and life can flourish into the universe. I fly all around and the Angel of Babylon flies with me we pass under the lake and over the huge stairway this place is beautiful.

09/07/16 22:00

The golden ramparts, the beautiful jade encrusted rock buttresses. All the plants, bejeweled, and the fog that surrounds. The mountainous enclave and headlands. I can see fires burning in the distance and smoke drifting. Man has built cities in the area, and monks have moved into the mountains to start training new religions of Gods. The old Goddess religions are gone. The Aryans are In India, and early Taoism (Daoism) is spreading in China. Buddhism will soon find its way from the mountains here in the Himalayas, the mythical Kunlun, and the Land of the Gods. These people are using the local hallucinogenic plants and fungi to mix with peaches and apricots to experiment with immortality. The Silk Road will provide a whole external population with religion and skilled shamanistic seers. Hell uses hallucinogens to produce the demons and Angels it requires. So, it's required for shamanistic people to see the immortals. Now with the use of an elixir, they are trying to produce an immortal. Angels of Hell will mix with these people to produce people who will live far beyond their time – 100's of years, some of which will turn into monsters, vampires, werewolves, shape shifters. And later the Sumerians with Babylon and The Angels of Babylon, one of whom I fly with now this whole vast area will produce more souls for Hell than were even imagined possible. Hell will grow exponentially leading to the Great Test where I was locked up for eternity. Now we watch as a large procession of people, soldiers, religious elite, and royalty are migrating out of India (These are the Aryan). They will pass through the mountains of the Hindu Kush, Himalayas. Then along the Kunlun Shan, the Mekong into what will be Vietnam. The north up the Xiang.

Eventually, up the Yangtze to Shanghai, where they will follow ocean currents to distant islands and into Ancient Japan. I believe these people will be the ones to follow while I seek the Mako. I fly to the mountain head lands and take in the sight. The numbers are staggering. 100,000's of people in groups of 1000's at a time. 100,000's of animals and millions of birds. All the while the Angels of people and the Angels of Hell. This migration is just unbelievable, fires spread as they more and wild animals more with and alongside the groups. My Babylonian Angel accompanies me now while I fly down to be with the peoples and animals. The Mako seeks truth. I seek only freedom. I move amongst the people, animals and their Angels. The Angels here give way for us as we fly their numbers don't mean anything to us. All Angels have a mission and cannot jeopardize their assignments to come into conflict with me. They cower and appear in a pusillanimous condition. The numbers of Angels here with humanity are truly multitudinous. Nevertheless, they all give way for us to travel with them. The Bitch from Hell flashes, as do I. We portal to the Far East coast. I am sure the Mako came this way to the ocean, Hell hunts her, but can't keep track of her wear-bouts because of her new duality minus the ghost of Hell. And now I can't fucking find her. However, I will, and that's why I brought this Bitch with me, she will find the Mako of that I am sure. She flashes, I follow we step out into Heaven, I am not sure why she has come here, and I, believe this might be a mistake; however, this duality is devious.

This is just fucked up, I stepped through the bubble from a portal with wings of Heaven. Accomplished with a Babylonian Bitch from

Hell into Heaven, and onto one of the golden streets our bodies are streaming smoke trails, and we cannot touch the golden streets but that sparks and smoke drifts from our every step. Bells are ringing all around as Heaven's Angels are gathering in great numbers to watch our passing down the road. Souls flicker and dance by. animals move on the grounds; rainbows appear in the sky as clouds pass and the sky turns dark in places. Stars and planetoids pass over. We continue to walk down the road. I am begging to remember this place. This is the road I walked with the Mako as we moved towards the crossroads. I am beginning to feel the importance of this plan by the Hell's Angel at my side. She is going to use her duality to empathetically possess the Mako's location from the positioning of the crossroads. Hell wants the Mako as much as I do. If anything can find her, this Bitch from Hell can. She can't replace the Mako, she isn't as strong a fighter as the Mako is however, the duality of a Hell's Angel is a devious thing to possess, and here in heaven, thus will either work or she will find out like I and the Mako did, that God holds sway what goes down here. What a beautiful place, green grass like no other, flowers and butterflies sparks of light, birds of all types, animals and rainbows. We walk on towards the crossroads, and then when we arrive from the direction of mission, we find stepping out of a portal, the Trinity, The Diaphanous speaks: "Stop Here".

I am your God; you will stop here at the crossroads. I believe that you are here to seek the Mako, Hell has sent the two of you here. I however have not invited either of you here. You cannot gain anything here and she knows that! A rod of lightning points straight at the Bitch of Babylon. She smiles at God, and she knows that the truth here is in the Fixer. She screams and strokes the street with her sword and draws a line on it. Smoke and a blue flame appear as she drags the sword. Fire is not possible here; she is tempting God to strike her down. Knowing full well he cannot. God does not care about her or me. He sends the golden bolt straight to her chest and speaks. You will not challenge me here or I will strike you down. The blue flame goes out the sword is withdrawn. She flashes; she has no portal nor

Heaven's wings to contend with. She reappears beside the transparent one, she dances around him. He begins to flicker but stands his ground. She flashes and reappears beside the Christ. God launches his golden rod straight through her. She is impaled on the rod and cannot move but she screams and stabs her sword into the Christ and drops her shield onto the street. Christ reaches out, pulls the golden rod from the chest of the Angel of Hell, as he begins to flicker and then a blue flame appears from his wound. The shield strikes the golden street, the portal disintegrates, this time pearls do not flood Heaven. This time, sand pours out and continues to pour out. The light from God becomes unbearable to look at.

Then his flash envelops the Christ and the source of sand both disappear. The Bitch screams and kicks sand and smoke and sparks and small blue flames lash out, she flashes and reappears beside me. Then God produces another rod and dims his brilliance. "The Fixer has his Will, the crossroads are not the place for you and, your spreading the sands of time here will be your undoing. I will not give into Hell; you will have to locate the Mako on your own. This is an Angel of Hell, and this Bitch is a duality and Hell sent here to locate the Mako, and she doesn't give a fuck if God can kill her and me. She is going to play a game and the stakes are high. In her mind, she deals the cards, picks them up, shuffles them then re-deals. Every card she deals out is fuck you, and fuck you, and fuck him, and then she finds the queen of diamonds. She screams at God and says Hell sent me here to lay calm on the Mako, I have a card in my mind, and you know what it is. I want to fill that card, and Hell doesn't give a fuck about the Pearl Nautilus, or the Fixer, or you either! If the Mako isn't stopped and stripped of the truth and her soul. So, let's play for real. I will play my card, let's see if you call my bluff. Come on God what the fuck kind of card have you got to trump this? She flashes and steps out of a portal high in Heaven and slowly a card from a deck of Tarot Cards drifts down to the golden crossroads. It's the Queen of Diamonds, The Hell's Bitch freezes everything. Heaven's Angels are in exceptionally large numbers around the group, all now frozen. Jesus Christ has been moved and can't absorb the pain; Gods armor will fall.

11/07/16 23:00

I look at her; I move close to her, she is frozen. Impossible, fucking impossible, I fucked up this Bitch for sure, she has frozen everything in Heaven for as far as I can see. She planned this before we even got here for fuck sakes. She is not even in her head. This is fucked up. The Transparent one is flashing and flickering, the diaphanous one is giving off a brilliance that is threatening to kill everything in Heaven. As I look at her I am looking at a vacant shell, she is not in there, both of her Ghosts of Hell are moving from one Heaven's Angel to another just as fast as they can. Gods armor is raining down to the ground, Heaven's Angels are drifting down onto the ground naked and they are crying. God's brilliance goes out and the one that walks on water returns to Gods side. The Bitch turns and looks at me, she has returned. God's Angels are everywhere, this looks like a total disaster. She growls, she rakes me with a clawed hand I scream and spin away and deal her a wound that won't heal. She doesn't realize my power, or she wouldn't have done that. She drops to the golden street. She vacates the dying Bitch and moves into a Heaven's Angel right in front of me. Her old body is a smoldering carcass. God touches her; the wings disappear. That's it she is totally helpless now. She is trapped in the mind of an Angel with no way to teleport or vacate. Hell needs you to complete the mission. I reach into her mind she has found the Mako, God gave her up to the Ghost of Hell, that I added to her. I pull the Ghost. God immediately beheads the Angel; I watch a spark lift to the Heavens. I watch as black smoke drifts as she is taken to Hell. I finally know where the Mako is.

I am still trying to take in what has happened as God points a golden staff at me. Fixer you brought her here. You will take that smoldering carcass with you when you leave. You will only to be allowed in Heaven again if you return with the Mako. Too many things have happened here with your unexpected arrival with this Babylonian Angel from Hell. I cannot forgive you for what has happened. Spilling the sands of time in Heaven caused time to pass without me present on Earth. When she speared the one that walks on water, my son on Earth died at the hand of a Centurion named Longinus. I had to give up the Mako in order to save my son and, clean up the sands of time, before more terrible this happened on Earth without me. And now you know that I have killed a Heaven's Angel in Heaven to stop a Hell's Angel from escaping with a ghost of Hell, bound to kill the Mako. All the while the Angels all around have all lost their armor from the freeze. All of this will end when you are on the frontline of the battle of Evermore. I assure you; you will be there with all of us. These things you do here cement your place in Hell and in Heaven. Go find the Mako, tell her all that has and will happen for the sands of time have not affected her. Let her find all the truths she seeks and then bring her home to Heaven, one last time before she goes to Hell. The truths she seeks are for Heaven & Earth. Hell will have to wait As the Fixer, I stride while smoke drifts from me. I gather the carcass. I look at all the Angels and I make my promise to God. I flash and step into and out of a portal into Hell.

REFERENCES

- Readers Digest

- Atlas of the World.

  ISBN # 0-89577-264-7

  All names of Countries, provinces, rivers, and lakes, I located in this book for spelling and geological location.

- The New Webster Encyclopedic Dictionary

  This book was indispensable for spelling, tense, usage, and meaning of various words. Also, used in the looking up of some Gods & Goddesses.

- Wikipedia.org. Where I looked up names of deities as given to me by the ghost in my head.

  This book and its contents are a work of fiction. No claim is made by its author to real events or any timeline.

EPILOGUE

I shine a light in the night

I place the full moon in the sky at night to control your passion. The ebb and flow contain a period of freedom to which your spirit refreshes. The light that shines from the moon dims as it becomes smaller. And in the night, you may become lost. So, without knowing, I place the stars in the heavens, in fixed places to give you reference. I place moving bodies in the stars to encourage you to move. The ones that come and go in your life, friends, and family they also shine a light in your life. Some fixed, some moving. But all must pass from sight. When they pass, the light from their life leaves your mind. I then take their light and add it to the stars in the heavens. So many you cannot count. So many you don't know. They are there to light your way even in the darkest night. Alas, you may find a night when the light cannot pass through the clouds. This is when you must depend on your faith. In the darkest night you look into the heavens, and no light appears. Faithfully, you know that in the heavens beats the heart of one that loves you more than any man. With that love you may find peace, and it will light up your soul.

Questions: 1-12:

1. Answer: Within days of ending my 30 + year marriage, I was discussing the situation with a close friend and extended family member. I began to relive my life and buried memories. I became overtaken by the presence of my deceased son.

2. The story spans 25,000, years. A mistake made by the gods starts a chain of events leading to The War of Evermore. The escape of a god locked up creates a new god and together they find the truth.

3. The central theme is, good and bad are opposite forces. These forces are never in balance. One is always threatening to overpower the other. Ultimately, the death of one will lead to the death of the other, they are codependent.

4. This book takes place on earth, in the heavens, and in Hell.

5. The main characters are The Fixer, and The Mako.

6. The Fixer is the most powerful Hell's Angel, a literal God.

7. The Mako is God produced by Heaven and the virtual power of the mind of Hell. The Mako is a Japanese name. Meaning (loosely) The Child of Truth. The Two "Gods" become codependent. The fixer wants to undo the mistakes of the Gods & Goddess. The Mako wants to expose all the truths of deception made by all the Gods.

8. This story has truly been an escape for my mind. There is so much deception in the world today. We live in a time on the brink of Armageddon. It is a universal theme amongst all to want to escape the chains that bind us, and to come face to face with the truth of our beliefs.

9. Today's society is watching too much TV, too much video, and playing to may games. We need to use our minds more to be creative, empower others, and build memories based on skillful achievements. Today is becoming truly a throwaway society. We are throwing away our lives on everything.

10. I write in the first person; therefore the reader gets to be right there in every situation. That's empowerment. The readers mind gets to see how things are, I leave enough holes in description to allow the reader to use his/her, imagination. That's creativity. I don't use gross language to describe events, allowing the reader to decide how much is enough? That's life skill ability.

11. The story is one derived from a life event that's all engrossing the loss of a life not lived. I took the story from the passing of a child; this is not a made-up event. I created a story from a story of extreme pain, heart break, and loss.

12. I want readers to be shaken up; I want them to go for a journey in their mind. I want them to experience what is all around, and what has been, and what can be finally I want the reader to find some truth in their beliefs.

13. I believe that the story was told to me while I was with my infant son in ICU. Soon after birth he was terminal moved to ICU, 15 hours later he passed. His mother wanted no name or funeral. I was devastated. At the time I couldn't handle the loss or the story he gave. For years I couldn't discuss the event. With the separation I felt the presence of the spirit and could smell the ICU. The spirit told me to write the story as I now had the life experience to do so, so I did it, I wrote it.

14. From the Epilogue: "I place the full moon in the night sky to control your passion. The ebb and flow contain a period of freedom to which your spirit refreshes."

Encyclopedia of Shinto — Kojiki — Ōkamuzumi
Izanagi, Izanami, Yomi, Japan
India — Hindu Insani, Iswara
Brahma d Vishnu
Tree of Heaven, Cosmic Tree. Karma Tree.
Ngadu-tree trunk.
Oedeypoor, Rajputana
Rajput — Gehlote — Sessodian clans. Iswara and Isani.
Mahadera-Iswara — tutelary divinity of Rajpoots in Mewar
"Gehlote adoration" Annals, Antiquities of Rajasthan
Saka-Sassanian-Sila roots of the royal myths of Indian
and Japanese tribes. Marrage of Inanna and Damuzi.
A Hymn of Sumer. A Tricontinental Nexus. Anatolia
Indus Valley.
Origin of the Aryan in India and their Migration to Ancient Japan.

東南アジア研究年報,52

PP. 21-28; 2011 / Similarities and common Saka-Sassanian-Sila
roots of the royal myths of Indian and Japanese tribes
Xiwang Mu. [Shikome. August Male.]
North Pakistan — Budapest.   The Eurasian Steppe, Mongolia.
A bride in China caries peach blossoms.
The peach — symbol of longevity, femal sexuality, purity d truth.
          — is the yin

Tarim Basin — Bronze Age.
The Peach as a Kami. a mother goddess   Momotaro, kamishibai.com
Shen, Phallus, Persian Apple.   Research page 2

Japan - early people - Jōmon - 21000 years ago.
Okinawan | Wang Mu. controls plagues and evil spirits. Motherly
         | figure to all gods of heaven.
Shinto - Kami-no-michi. ⌐Fabled Garden of the Western Paradise - Kunlun Mountains
                        |Tibet and Xijiang.
Amaterasu.- Shining in heaven│Kunlun range - part of the
                              │Silk Road. - China-Persia

The Kunlin mountians /Uttar Pradesh.
The Hindu Kush Mountian Range
Old Khmer (Old Cambodian
Sanskrit - Śailarāja kings of the mountian.
Trans-Gangetic Indra.   Hallucinogenic
Sailendra Thalassocracy
The Kunlin is lavished with in paradisaical detail
Gem like rocks, towering cliffs of jasper or jade.
exotic jeweled plants bizarrely formed and colored
fungi and The Eight Imortals visiting with.
Xi Wangmu + Yu Shi Sun Wukong Tai Di
with golden ram parts. The lake of Gems.
Peaches produce Imortality every 6000 yrs.
The gods must drink an elixer made from peaches every 3000 yrs.
A peach with a leaf attached symbolizes the union of the heart to tounge
hence - truth.
Moon goddess Legend of Hou-yi Chang-e and Xiwang Mu's peaches.
The Golden Peaches of Samarkand
The kingdom of Samarkand.
Seeds, bark and leaves contain low levels of cyanide. Therapeutic
for cancer. Powerfull dose of Vitamin A.   Research Page 1